THORNTON'S LUCK

*How America Almost
Lost the Mexican-American War*

LAMONT WOOD

LONE
STAR
BOOKS
GUILFORD, CONNECTICUT

To Louise

LONE STAR BOOKS

An imprint and registered trademark of Globe Pequot

Distributed by NATIONAL BOOK NETWORK

Copyright © 2017 by Lamont Wood

British Library Cataloguing-in-Publication Information available

Library of Congress Cataloging-in-Publication Data available

ISBN 978-1-4930-2555-8 (paperback)
ISBN 978-1-4930-2833-7 (e-book)

♾™ The paper used in this publication meets the minimum requirements of American National Standard for Information Sciences—Permanence of Paper for Printed Library Materials, ANSI/ NISO Z39.48-1992.

Contents

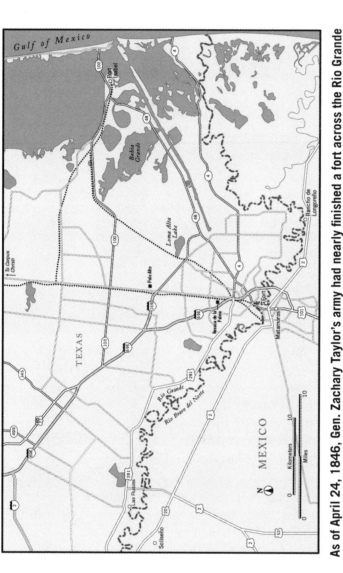

As of April 24, 1846, Gen. Zachary Taylor's army had nearly finished a fort across the Rio Grande from Matamoros. He had also established a base and port at Point Isabel, but had no way to protect the road between the fort and the base. That night he sent a patrol west to Las Rusias under Capt. Seth B. Thornton to see if a Mexican force had crossed. The next morning the patrol was ambushed at an undetermined point on the riverbank east of Las Rusias, triggering a declaration of war. General Taylor thereafter retreated to Point Isabel with most of his force and his supply wagons. When returning he fought the battles of Palo Alto and Resaca de la Palma. The exact course of the river is largely conjectural. The dotted lines indicate the main roads that existed in 1846, while the rest of the infrastructure, shown for reference, is modern. Port Isabel was then called Point Isabel. Credit: Alena Pearce

Preface

THE MEXICAN-AMERICAN WAR ENDED WELL FOR THE UNITED STATES, largely shaping the nation as it now exists. The US has since contributed a great deal to shaping the modern world. But that war began disastrously for the US with the now-forgotten Thornton Affair, the incident that was also the official cause of the war. What's also forgotten is that the disaster could easily have spread to destroy half the US Army as it existed at the time, dashing any hope of a successful military campaign, and ultimately precluding the formation of today's United States.

As this book will show, what happened that day was a direct product of the bad luck and stubbornness of Seth B. Thornton, captain, 2nd Regiment, US Dragoons. Yet what exactly happened to him, why, and even where, has remained obscure, despite the pivotal nature of the event.

For decades historians have quoted, expounded on, and been led astray by the vague, error-ridden, self-serving reports submitted by the two surviving senior officers, Captain Thornton and his second-in-command, Capt. W. J. Hardee. Their reports established that the Thornton Affair did happen, and that a patrol was ambushed and destroyed by Mexican forces on the north side of the Rio Grande. That was sufficient for a declaration of war on Mexico. But further details have remained elusive.

It turns out that both Captain Thornton and Captain Hardee later had to explain to military courts (convened in Matamoros, Mexico) what happened in detail. But the government clerks wrote on both sides of the paper, the ink bled through, ran, or both, and the results were only occasionally legible. As a result, no one appears to have consulted their testimony for more than a century and a half. Meanwhile, historians continued to be led astray by their original reports.

The author was able to get scanned copies of the court files from the US National Archives and Records Administration and blow them up on a large screen. It proved possible to work through them, line by line, and establish the bulk of what the clerks had originally written. (Getting used to their handwriting and phrasing was also helpful.) The result was a clear, blow-by-blow account of what happened. But it also made clear that things could easily have turned out differently, and Captain Thornton could have avoided his bad luck. But it's also clear that had he done so the results would have been very bad luck for the US Army and probably for the United States.

This book will additionally examine how various threads—including Thornton's personality—wove themselves together to create what we now call history.

The author has chosen to translate *caudillo* and *cacique* as used to refer to Mexican leaders like Santa Anna and Arista, as "warlord," since war and reliance on military solutions was an integral part of Mexican politics at the time.

For those on the United States side of the conflict, the author has also chosen to use "US" instead of "American," as their US nationality was about the only thing a lot of "Americans" had in common at the time. The war would extend that nationality to about a tenth of the 1846 Mexican population.

At the time, the US dollar and the Mexican peso were of equal value and interchangeable. The $ (dollar sign) refers to both or either.

The author would like to thank Douglas A. Murphy, PhD, historian and administrator at the Palo Alto National Battlefield, for numerous pointers and insights; Jerrilynn Eby MacGregor, secretary of the Stafford County (Virginia) Historical Society, for insights on Thornton's origins; Tim O'Donnell for his patient translation efforts; and literary agent Jeff Herman for undertaking a project that involved understanding that the past is prologue to the present.

CHAPTER 1

The Upriver Reconnaissance

IT WAS EIGHT O'CLOCK[1] IN THE MORNING. THAT MEANT THAT CAPT. Seth B. Thornton of the 2nd Regiment of US Dragoons had only four hours to get back to base with what he'd learned.

If he turned back in the next few minutes he could still make it. The base was at least twenty-five road miles away, following the winding river, but his men were all well-mounted on government-issued horses, and by trotting[2] most of the way—covering eight or nine miles an hour—they could make it back by the noon deadline he'd been given. True, the horses had been up most of the night, as had the men, but they could rest when they got back.

The problem was that he hadn't learned anything, and had no information to bring back, and there was no guarantee that he would learn anything in the next half hour or so, when he truly would have to turn back.

On the other hand, what if there was nothing to learn? At what point should he decide that there was nothing to report, and turn back? The question must have arisen anew every time he went around a bend in the track, hemmed in by chaparral thicket just high enough to block the visibility of a man on horseback, and saw nothing ahead.

He was supposed to go to a place called Las Rusias, twenty-seven miles from camp, before turning back, but it was looking like he would not be able to get there and return by noon. Since the goal was out of reach, the question of turning back demanded a fresh answer from one moment to the next.

Yet, he kept running into hints that there was indeed something important to be learned, and he might find it around the next bend in the road. But so far he simply had nothing tangible to report.

But as far as intangibles go, what he had learned three miles (or so) back down the road might have satisfied a lot of men in his situation. It had certainly satisfied Chipito, his local guide, who thereupon took fright and fled. But Captain Thornton was stubborn. Anyway, it could be that Chipito had just been frightened by yet another rumor, and rumors were endemic here in the disputed territory. So Captain Thornton pressed on.

It was Saturday, April 25, 1846, on a cart track cutting through an interminable, and largely impassable, chaparral thicket on the north bank of the meandering Rio Grande, between twenty-five and thirty miles west of the Mexican city of Matamoros. Captain Thornton, twenty-nine, had been in combat before, and had survived a harrowing shipwreck that probably eclipsed anything he'd experienced in combat. In the meantime he'd barely held on to his career in the army while feuding with a superior officer. His life experiences had taught him to be stubborn. And today his stubbornness would lead to an unmitigated debacle for him and his command, as well as start a major war. But it would also save the US Army from disaster and put the United States on a path to becoming a leading nation-state.

The previous night he had been summoned by the commander of the expedition, Bvt. Brig. Gen. Zachary Taylor, to the general's tent inside the sizable but unfinished earthen fort the US forces were building on the north side of the Rio Grande opposite Matamoros. In fact, the base was called the Camp Opposite Matamoros, since there was no fort yet. (Later, after the earthwork was finished and then successfully defended, it would be called Fort Brown. A city would spring up to the north of it, called Brownsville.) General Taylor commanded a force of fewer than four thousand men, grandly called the Army of Occupation, sent to exert the US claim, inherited with the annexation of Texas, that the Rio Grande was the US border.

Taylor's Army of Occupation had arrived March 28 after marching south from a coastal camp near the then-hamlet and smugglers' roost of Corpus Christi, Texas. The Mexicans had a sizable garrison in Matamoros, but for almost a month the two sides were content to exchange frosty denunciations, as they had other things on their minds besides conducting a border war.

The first priority of the US commanders was to finish building a fort around their camp, from which they could glimpse—over the trees that crowded the intervening river bottomland—the spires of Matamoros's cathedral hardly a mile away. Their engineers had laid out a monumental, elongated-star-shaped earthwork, enclosing two acres, with walls nine and a half feet high and fifteen feet thick behind a dry moat eight and a half feet deep. Thousands of cubic yards of alluvial dirt had to be excavated and moved by hundreds of enlisted men using hand tools, and it was taking weeks. Once the fort was ready, serious operations could begin.

The Mexican commanders' priority was to wait for the political situation in Mexico City to become clear. Gen. Mariano Paredes had recently installed himself as president during recent unrest triggered by the US government's clumsy attempt to buy northern Mexico and the Mexican public's suspicions that the previous junta might actually sell it. Gen. Mariano Arista, a cultured warlord who believed that bribes trumped bloodshed, had previously controlled the Mexican army's El División Norte (which included Matamoros). But he was on the outs because he had not supported General Paredes's coup. However, General Arista's replacement turned out to be unacceptable to the locals—something about his penchant for brutality.

But even before the latest round of unrest the region had been a restive federalist hotbed, and at times had been in open rebellion against the incumbent centralist government. After General Santa Anna enhanced his personal power by replacing federalism with centralism in 1835, it developed that states on the Mexican periphery favored federalism and the self-government it gave them. Meanwhile, the centrally located ones, who had the ear of the government, favored centralism. Disenchantment on the periphery included the famous 1836 secession of Texas and the less famous 1841–1848 secession of Yucatan.

Likewise, south of Texas, the northeast Mexican states of Coahuila, Nueva Leon, and Tamaulipas had also seceded from Mexico in

1840, becoming the República del Río Grande (Rio Grande Republic). After some inconclusive fighting, General Arista had moved decisively to restore order through the use of strategic bribery.[3]

Six years later, despite the US incursion, the public mood along the Rio Grande was again so restive that the Mexican commanders dared not gather supplies using the usual methods (i.e., expropriations and IOUs). By all accounts they were barely able to keep their army in the field even before a hostile force had installed itself across the river.

The US force, meanwhile, had its own busy seaport and a wagon train three miles long, and anyway paid for everything in cash. They had traded casualties with bushwhackers upon arrival, but this was the West, and you expected that. There was an upsurge of desertion when they got to the Rio Grande, but that was assumed to be because there was now some-place to which a disaffected soldier could desert. (The Corpus Christi encampment, and the intervening territory they marched through, was basically a wasteland.) The Mexican authorities had distributed leaflets encouraging desertion by US soldiers who were Catholics, or who were just fed up with soldiering. Literacy not being a given, printed propaganda may not have had much impact. Meanwhile, there were pretty young ladies who were in the habit of bathing nude on the south bank of the river, in plain sight of the Camp Opposite Matamoros less than one hundred yards away on the north side of the river, and they often had difficulty remembering where they left their clothes. They may have had more impact.

And then, with the fort still unfinished, word came that General Arista had been restored—and he was going to strike north.

Later in the campaign a New Orleans businessman visited both General Arista and General Taylor at their respective headquarters. At Arista's he found something out of a fairytale, with his office in a large, colorful tent, with obsequious staff officers in glittering uniforms, live music, and costly ornamental furniture topped with heavy silver services. Outside were parked beautifully caparisoned horses, plus heaps of sup-plies beyond the imagination of the private soldier. Business meetings involved time-wasting pomp and ceremony with posturing courtiers.

In the US camp he had trouble spotting General Taylor's tent since they all looked alike. It turned out to be the one pitched in the shade. There, Taylor was using chests as a table, and a box as a chair. (He preferred not to wear his dress uniform, and generally had the air of a rich farmer who didn't need this job—which was the case.) A plainly dressed servant came when summoned. He served water.[4]

Captain Thornton reached General Taylor's tent about 9:00 p.m. on the 24th and was told to take two companies of dragoons and go upriver (i.e., west) nine leagues (twenty-seven miles) "examining the country" to see if the enemy had crossed anywhere in that interval, and if so with what force, and if they had artillery. At the nine-league point there was a settlement called Las Rusias (The Silver-Gray Mares, or alternately The Russian Women). Exactly why General Taylor picked Las Rusias to be scouted is not recorded. Presumably it was in the vicinity of a known river crossing. He wanted Thornton to be back by noon the next day, i.e., in fifteen hours. (Two other companies were sent on a similar errand downriver. They encountered nothing.)

They were both professional military men, immersed in the methods and technology of 1846, and both knew what the schedule implied. A horse walks at four miles an hour and trots at eight or nine miles an hour. (Galloping with government horses was reserved for special occasions.) On the road, it was considered good practice to periodically alternate between walking and trotting, the variation being refreshing for both horses and riders. There were elaborate formulas for how much walking and trotting a column of horsemen needed to do in order to cover a given distance in a given time, but the upshot was that they could expect to average six miles an hour.

So they were being called on to make a round trip totaling fifty-four miles in fifteen hours. At six miles per hour they should have been able to push on for ninety miles in fifteen hours, so their assignment was, in theory, not a problem.

But they would be moving at night, through unknown terrain, in disputed territory. Resting at intervals would also be desirable, especially considering that it was 9:00 p.m. and the men and horses had already been up all day.

"The General desires that you move with the utmost caution, keeping out advanced and flank guards, and taking the greatest care not to be drawn into an ambuscade," continued the written version of his orders. ("Ambuscade" was the contemporary term for "ambush.") "You will hold yourself ready to cut through any armed party that may be in your way."

General Taylor also told him to, "Thoroughly examine every place with a few men, whenever there was a possibility of an ambush being made before he committed his command. It would be better to rush and sacrifice a few than the whole."

The instructions, in practice, meant he was to dismount and check suspicious choke-points on foot. That would impose repeated delays. "Examining the country" meant the patrol would need to interrogate everyone they came across, imposing more delays. Maintaining six miles an hour was, therefore, out of the question. If they could maintain four miles an hour on the outbound leg, and not get bogged down by any incidents when halted, and then head straight back, without stopping, after they reached Las Rusias, they might get back in time—but those were big ifs.

Meanwhile, they were dragoons, not cavalry. That meant they rode horses but were equipped and trained to fight on foot, like infantry. The regiment had accumulated a variety of firearms since its founding ten years earlier and it's not certain what Captain Thornton's men were carrying that day. Candidates include a muzzle-loading carbine, or the deceptively modern Hall carbine whose cartridge chamber tilted up so it could be loaded without a ramrod. (The chamber never precisely fit the bore, leaking fire, smoke, and muzzle velocity with each shot.[5]) They had also been issued the Colt Paterson five-shot revolver, a first-generation multi-shot pistol that was, however, clumsy, unsafe, and required special tools to reload. Since Captain Thornton was recorded as telling the men to check the priming of their pistols, they may have been relying on conventional flintlocks. They also had swords, so the talk of cutting their way through the enemy was not, strictly speaking, hyperbole.

Whatever exact firearms they had, firing them unsteadily from horseback was unlikely to produce decisive results. Then, having fired their weapons, they'd have great difficulty reloading while in the saddle. So if they had to fight in the saddle they would end up using their swords.

But they would be at a severe disadvantage if they got into a mounted fight with real cavalry. Every Mexican cavalry company (regardless of type) included at least a dozen lancers, who carried an eight-foot lance topped with a steel point.[6] (Under the point hung a little red pennant that, from a distance, looked like a streak of blood.) In the very likely event that Thornton's men couldn't drive off the lancers with their gunfire, they could be speared by the lancers while they struggled to reload. Meanwhile, the lancers would be safely out of reach of the dragoons' swords.

Worse, the typical Mexican cavalry formation was an equal mix of heavy cavalry (with metal breastplates and helmets, mounted on heavy horses, intended for frontal assaults), light cavalry (without the armor, on light horses picked for speed, intended to scout, harass, and pursue the enemy) and dragoons. (Prior to his most recent exile, Santa Anna's personal escort cavalry regiment back in Mexico City had been a purely heavy unit whose polished bronze officer helmets were crested with flowing horse manes and tri-color plumes, and were trimmed in jaguar pelts.) Against the heavy cavalry Captain Thornton's men would be (after firing their weapons) unarmored men sword-fighting with armored men. Against the light cavalry and dragoons there was more hope—if they weren't overwhelmingly outnumbered and if they could stay away from those lancers.

On the other hand, if the dragoons dismounted and fought as infantry they could defend themselves against any kind of cavalry pretty much indefinitely. It may sound counter-intuitive, but to hold off cavalry all infantry had to do was stand shoulder-to-shoulder. (Firing their weapons would also help.) The oncoming horses would flinch from colliding with a wall of standing men, and turn aside. That had been demonstrated on many European battlefields. But if, amid the shooting and chaos, just standing there proved too counter-intuitive for the defenders and they flinched and scattered, the cavalry would chase them down like rabbits. That, too, had been demonstrated on many European battlefields.

But for Captain Thornton a successful defense was not the issue. If he stopped and fought, successfully or otherwise, he would not be making progress back to base. He was supposed to gather information, and his orders implied that he was to accept the risk of fighting mounted, at a disadvantage, if that's what it took to bring back the information. Charging straight at them, hoping they would flinch and give way, was about the only thing that might work. And so he talked of cutting his way through. If he had any reservations during his meeting with General Taylor, Thornton kept them to himself—he'd been given an order, not a debate topic. (Later, after things turned out disastrously, he had a few things to say.)

But the fact that Taylor sent two companies indicated that he attached considerable importance to the reconnaissance, and that he suspected it might run into trouble. Of the five under-strength regiments (and one full-strength battalion) in General Taylor's little army, the 2nd Dragoons was the only mounted unit. It had seven companies on hand, so by giving Captain Thornton two he was effectively giving him almost one-third of the force's mounted troops.

Captain Thornton was the commander of Company F of the 2nd Dragoons. For this patrol he was also given Company C. At the time, regiments were the basic administrative units of the US Army (and most other armies). Each regiment was commanded by a colonel, assisted by a lieutenant colonel and a major or two. Each regiment typically had ten companies, designated A through K (skipping J to avoid visual confusion with I). Each had about one hundred men, commanded by a captain, assisted by one or two lieutenants.

But this was still officially peacetime, and the US Army, although deployed in disputed territory in the face of an armed enemy, retained its peacetime headcount as specified by Congress in 1842 retrenchment legislation: a maximum of forty-two privates per infantry and artillery company, and fifty for each company of dragoons.[7] (The army as a whole was also low on officers, and there were regiments commanded by senior captains.) Meanwhile, three of the regiment's companies had had to be sent to the Texas frontier to watch the Indians, leaving only seven on hand to confront the Mexican army, whose composition reflected that nation's rich heritage of horsemanship.

Of course, there had been the usual attrition, including illness, expired enlistments, and desertions. So when Captain Thornton moved out with two companies he only had fifty-one troopers, plus local guide Chipito, three officers, and himself, giving the patrol a headcount of fifty-six. (Incidentally, two companies acting together was called a squadron, and the patrol was called a squadron in some documents.)

Of the three[8] other officers, second in command was the head of Company C, Capt. William J. Hardee, twenty-nine, an 1838 West Point graduate from Georgia. He was a tall, sinewy man who was finicky about his appearance, finicky about what he ate, and (as it turned out) finicky about his reputation. Thornton was only six months older but was senior to Hardee by three years, being made captain in 1841 (after being a lieutenant for five years) to Hardee's 1844 (after being a lieutenant for six years). But if you count the time he spent in West Point, Hardee had actually been in the army longer, becoming a cadet in 1834 and becoming a second lieutenant only after enduring life at the military academy.

Thornton, on the other hand, was directly commissioned as a second lieutenant in 1836 after having attended two different liberal arts colleges. He was described as having a small, even delicate, build, to the point that people thought he was dying of some condition and was getting through the day on sheer force of will. He consistently denied that anything was wrong.

Both had served in Florida during the Second Seminole War, but Thornton had seen considerably more action than Hardee, who managed to get himself sent overseas for a year to attend a French riding school at government expense.

Whatever the reason, the two generally got along like oil and water. Captain Hardee would soon be writing a report that blamed that day's disaster on Captain Thornton. Before the end of the war that started that day Hardee would also try, and fail, to get Thornton thrown out of the army for drunkenness.

On this day Thornton stationed Hardee at the very rear of the column, implying later that this was the standard assignment of a patrol's second-in-command. Actually it was the proper place of the commander, to keep men from dropping out, but Thornton had the enemy to worry about, so he delegated that task. Hardee didn't complain—although it was about the only thing he would not later complain about.

Riding with Captain Hardee at the rear, at least initially, was the sole lieutenant in his company, Lt. George T. Mason, twenty-seven, an 1842 West Point graduate from Virginia. Lieutenant Mason was also the great-grandson of George Mason, coauthor with James Madison of the Bill of Rights. Fort Mason, Texas, and then the surrounding Mason County, about a hundred miles northwest of Austin, would later be named after him. At West Point he was known for his swordsmanship. Today, that skill would not save his life.

Also in the patrol was 2nd Lt. Elias Kent Kane Jr., twenty-four, an 1841 West Point graduate from Illinois where his father, Elias K. Kane, had written the state's first constitution. (The elder Kane, who had died in 1835, had also been a US senator, and was the namesake of Kane County, just west of Chicago.) Kane was the sole lieutenant in Captain Thornton's company.

Photography was leading-edge technology in 1846, and Captain Hardee is the only one of the four known to have had his photo taken, and that much later, after he became a Confederate general. His second wife also commissioned a painted portrait during the war. The images show wavy dark hair, a wooly mustache, a trimmed beard, a narrow face, a chiseled nose, an impeccably tailored uniform, and overall an air of self-conscious dignity.

As for Captain Thornton, a front-line journalist who interviewed him during the coming months spoke of his "small stature and delicate constitution," and also of his apparent lack of luck.[9]

Captain Thornton had the patrol leave camp immediately. Captain Hardee had patrolled upriver before, and on his advice Thornton led the two companies up the river road fifteen miles to a ranch with a front yard big enough for them to rest in. Presumably Thornton wanted his men to get some sleep so they could be alert when they headed into unknown territory. On the march the men were told to maintain silence and keep their spurs and swords from jingling.

The road amounted to a corridor through a random succession of dense, man-high thickets called chaparral, which blocked both movement and visibility. At the rest stop they were able to maintain security simply by posting sentinels a hundred yards in either direction on the road. Since there was no other route through which they could be approached, they were safe from ambush—for the moment. The men, however, were told to keep their horses' bridles in their hands, in case they needed to mount up fast.

Chipito left the patrol during this period, but returned before they were back on the road. Later, Captain Thornton wondered about this.

They moved out again about dawn. The terrain was as constricted as ever. Normally they would have sent out flankers to ride parallel to the road, to flush out any ambushes, but that was not practical here. Having a rear guard also seemed pointless. Thornton did send out an advance guard, consisting of Chipito, two privates, and Sgt. George Lenz of Company F, who, despite his Germanic name, was the patrol's Spanish interpreter.

There would have been a ranch or house of some sort about every mile, and they stopped at every one asking if the residents had heard news of the Mexican army. The replies they got all sounded like rumors.

"Some would say that they had crossed, and others that they had not," Lieutenant Kane, who was riding alongside Captain Thornton at the front of the main body, would testify later.

Presumably, they were all just saying whatever they thought these armed men wanted to hear, and the results were the equivalent of random noise.

It went on like this for about ten miles. At one point they were joined by a bystander, who was friendly enough to want to tag along and show them the way. When the terrain permitted Chipito would ride off to the left (i.e., toward the river) as if to check on something, Thornton later recalled. At the time he thought nothing of it.

Then they came to a group of houses where three men were gathered in the front. Chipito got into a whispered conversation with them—Sergeant Lenz, the interpreter, was not involved. The conversation got more and more excited, and went on for as long as ten minutes.

Finally, Chipito turned to Thornton—and said a large Mexican force was waiting about a mile and a half ahead. The patrol must turn back, as the road remained narrow and they would not be able to retreat when they met the enemy. And if they went on he, Chipito, would not be going with them. He said something about not wanting his throat slit.

Chipito (called Chipita in some sources) was presumably a smuggler by trade, as he was an associate of the founder of Corpus Christi, adventurer "Colonel" H. L. Kinney, and reportedly helped him break out of jail in Matamoros at one point. Chipito was described as in the prime of life, of middling height, with broad shoulders and muscles like whipcords, dark piercing eyes, prominent forehead, and brushy eyebrows. An experienced frontiersman, he was said to be able to ride his startlingly skinny horse from the Rio Grande to Corpus Christi in a day and a night.[10]

Whatever threats, promises, or bribes that Captain Thornton used to try to get him to go on, they didn't work, and Chipito turned back. The bystander who had previously joined the patrol went with him.

At this point Thornton began to suspect that Chipito was a double agent, and that he'd led them into a trap. At least, that's what he said later. At the time, he pressed on, as if he saw Chipito as honest but easily frightened.

"It may be said I ought to have returned from this point and reported to the commanding general what I had learned," he testified several months later. "But I submit to the court whether I had yet gained reliable information on which to base a report. I had seen nothing of an enemy and no signs of one, and reports previously made to us, in a similar manner, have proven to be so totally incorrect that I dared not rely on these. I had learned nothing either of the enemy's strength or composition, and, in a word, the object of my expedition had not been accomplished."

In other words, he decided to be thorough—and stubborn.

Captain Hardee was still in the rear. The fifty-five-man patrol was riding in a single file, so assuming five yards per horseman Hardee was at least 250 yards behind Thornton and was unlikely to have heard a word that was said. Nevertheless, he gathered the impression that the bystanders who Thornton had been interrogating had all agreed that the Mexicans had crossed the river, and that they had now convinced Chipito of the fact—but that Thornton was not buying any of it.

Back in camp he'd heard Thornton say that to fight the Mexicans he wanted his men armed only with whips. Thornton did not take the

Mexicans seriously, he decided—and would say as much in the report he sent back the next day.

Riding alongside Captain Thornton, Lieutenant Kane got the impression that Thornton was taking the Mexicans quite seriously indeed. After Chipito left, Thornton passed the word through the command that the enemy could be nearby and the men must be ready for action, Kane later testified. The men were to take off their greatcoats and tie them to their saddles. They were told to sling and load their carbines, and to check the priming of their pistols.

Meanwhile, Lieutenant Mason was pulled from the rear and put in charge of the advance guard, which was reinforced with about ten more men. He was told to stay a quarter-mile in front of the main body of the patrol, and to fire and then retreat to the main body if he did encounter an enemy force.

"I fear an ambuscade," Captain Thornton told Lieutenant Mason.

They moved out. The enemy was supposed to be a mile and a half ahead.

They went that far and encountered nothing.

This surely seemed like another invitation to turn back. The enemy was supposed to be here and they weren't. It was just another rumor. There was nothing to report.

Instead he pressed on—perhaps another half-mile, perhaps another mile and a half, depending on who made the estimate. Still no enemy was discovered. It was 8:00 a.m. and they would have to turn back soon.

Now, surely, would be a good time.

They came to a point where the road curved sharply right, away from the river, around a collection of open fields they would later refer to as "the plantation," although there was no mention of anything growing there. There was a horse-proof fence on the perimeter of the plantation, and its interior was subdivided by smaller fences. The plantation extended along the river for several hundred yards, and spread to the right (i.e., north) of the river about two hundred yards. At the far end they could see some houses (called "huts" in some accounts) and a gate with sliding bars. They could see that there were several people in the fields.

Captain Hardee figured the plantation covered about three hundred acres. That was probably a carefully considered number, since it would be about half a "section" of 640 acres (i.e., a square mile), which was the basic unit of land defined by the US Public Land Survey System. A section would have been a unit that those with rural backgrounds (i.e., most of them) would have been familiar with.

Although they could look into the plantation, their horses could not penetrate the perimeter fence, and the dense chaparral growth on either side of the fence made jumping the fence with their horses impractical. They later referred to it as Rancho de Carricitos (Little Cane Ranch). They understood that it was just short of their goal, Las Rusias.

As the road began to curve away from the river and around the plantation on their left, Thornton decided to counter-march the unit, so the rear of the patrol was now the front, and return to the point where the road encountered the plantation. There was a path at that point that led toward the river. Here he sent a sergeant and eight men to the riverbank to look up and down the river for activity, and to see if they could enter the plantation.

While waiting for them to return, Hardee approached Thornton to ask what was going on. Instead of giving his appreciation of the situation, Thornton just told him to return to his post, as the enemy might appear at any moment.

The scouts returned—they could see a mile up and down the river, but spotted nothing. Nor could they find a way into the plantation. (You'd think the fence would not run into the river and so they could slip around the end of the fence at the riverbank. Elsewhere in the files, though, testimony describes the riverbank as too boggy to support a horse.)

Having seen no activity on the river, this surely would have been a good time to turn back. He could still get back in time, and could reasonably report that there was nothing to report.

But then Captain Hardee heard from one of his men that a Mexican horseman had appeared up the road, in the direction toward which they had previously been headed. The horseman had disappeared off the road on a path that led away from the river.

They proceeded back up the road to the point where the horseman had disappeared. Captain Thornton examined the northbound path that the vanished rider took, away from the main road. From the tracks on the path Thornton decided that as many as five hundred horseman had recently ridden down that path. Very likely, he decided, they were on their way to get behind the patrol and cut them off from their base.

At this point he told Lieutenant Kane that they might have to cut their way through to get back to camp. "He would hack his way through the enemy and I was to follow him to prevent the opening he might make from being closed, whether he fell or not," Kane later testified.

Captain Thornton meanwhile led the patrol down the path, away from the river road, following the hoof prints. The path left the thicket and headed across a marshy prairie. Visibility opened up—and still no enemy was seen. Meanwhile, there was a rain shower.

After maybe ten minutes of seeing nothing, Thornton apparently decided that following the trail was a waste of time—and time was something he was rapidly running out of. But there had definitely been people at that plantation back on the river. Maybe they had seen something. He had the patrol do an about-face and return to the road, and resume their original direction, up the road, with the plantation on the left, still visible across the fence.

Upon getting back to the road, Captain Hardee (who'd been in the rear, but was now in front thanks to the counter-march to return from the prairie) noted that just enough rain had fallen to wash away the old tracks—but now there were new tracks on the road. Someone had ridden a horse there in both directions while the patrol was on the side path. That seemed suspicious to him, but he was not able to alert Captain Thornton, who was at the other end of the column.

Indeed, after the unit had resumed forward motion on the main road, Thornton had ridden ahead to the advance guard, stopped it, and told Lieutenant Mason to send the interpreter and one man to the plantation houses to the left, to see if they could learn anything. For access he apparently meant for them to make a gap in the fence that skirted the road. Mason, however, suggested that they just follow the road, as he thought it would soon turn left and reach the plantation's gate.

The move turned out to be a catastrophically bad idea—or, it might have been the only thing that could have saved their lives.

As predicted, the road soon curved to the left and passed, on the left side of the road, the entrance to the plantation, which was blocked by a gate with draw bars.

They slid away the draw bars that closed the gate. Captain Thornton took the interpreter and headed—at a gallop—toward the plantation houses, about two hundred yards away, where he could see several mounted men. It was not clear if they were armed. When he got about halfway to the houses the horsemen suddenly rode off.

Meanwhile, back on the road, the main body of the patrol came around the left curve and unexpectedly ran into the advance guard, which was gathered at the gate. Had there been more visibility they probably would have stopped on the main road and maintained their distance from the advance guard.

After the horsemen took flight from the houses, Captain Thornton beckoned for the advance guard to follow him into the field. He made that gesture without looking back, and without noticing that the main body had caught up and had merged with the advance guard. Responding to his gesture, the advance guard followed him into the field, and then the main body followed the advance guard. No guard was left at the gate, and no scouts were sent farther up the road.

As a body, they soon caught up with Thornton, and followed him the rest of the way to the houses. Thornton remarked that he had not wanted them to do that, but said nothing else and gave no orders to correct the situation. He then told a sergeant to take one man, follow the fleeing horsemen, and bring back one.

"And don't shoot him," he concluded.

The rest of the troopers got to the huts—and order evaporated. Some got water for their horses, some lay on the ground as if it were nap time, some slumped in their saddles, some lit their pipes, and some began to search the huts with Lieutenant Kane. Engrossed in his intelligence gathering, Captain Thornton paid no attention. Very likely they were all operating in a haze of fatigue.

The troopers found an old man in one of the houses and brought him to Captain Thornton, who started asking questions. Meanwhile, one of the fleeing horseman was collared and also brought back for questioning.

They had been on the plantation grounds for perhaps five minutes.

Then, there was a commotion from the direction of the plantation entrance that they had just passed through. Captain Thornton looked up.

"Jesus Christ there's thousands of them!" he yelled. "Draw your sabers men, and charge!"

CHAPTER 2

Stranger to Luck

CAPTAIN THORNTON MADE IT TO RANCHO DE CARRICITOS ON THE morning of April 25, 1846, only because he was too stubborn to turn back. Indeed, what is known of his life story up to that morning is a tale of a man who had learned to counter bad luck with stubbornness. He was stubborn enough to get an army commission despite being small and sickly. Then he was stubborn enough to cling to floating debris for six days after the steamer on which he was a passenger exploded and sank. That didn't help his health, but he stubbornly stayed in the army. His stubbornness led to a feud with another officer who tried to keep him from being promoted. The feud stubbornly played out in two courts-martial and one court of inquiry, but Thornton clung to his career in the army like he had clung to that raft. The Thornton Affair might not have happened otherwise.

Seth Brett Thornton was born May 28, 1815, apparently on family property in Orange County, Virginia. He was raised on his father's estate "Rumford" in Stafford County, Virginia,[1] on the north bank of the Rappahannock River, about two miles downstream (i.e., east) of Fredericksburg. (It was also just downstream from Ferry Farm, George Washington's by then derelict boyhood home.[2]) He was the youngest of the four children of George Washington Thornton (1778–1816) and Mary Randolph Thornton (1785–1865) who had gotten married in 1805.[3]

His father died intestate when Seth Brett was less than two years old. A guardian was appointed for the children and there were disputes about the management of the estate, leading to several lawsuits.[4]

One of his older sisters (Mary Goode Thornton Scott, subsequently of Pensacola) later told a genealogist that his family was able to send Seth to two different liberal arts colleges: Kenyon College in Ohio in 1830, and Trinity College in Connecticut in 1832. (At the latter his sister reported that he came into contact with the poet Lydia Sigourney, then at the height of her fame.) But his health failed after two years and he had to return home, give up books, and rest.[5]

The family sold Rumford about 1833, meaning there was no farm to go home to. (The estate house has not survived.[6]) He instead went to his father's relatives in Kentucky. After two years at leisure, "finding that he was not strong enough to pursue a course of professional study, he obtained a commission in the army," she said. How it was that not being strong enough to, for instance, read law, meant that he was fit to be an army officer went unsaid. Perhaps he had vision problems that produced migraines when he read too long. Such a "weakness" would not preclude field service. But his sister also reported that he was "by no means physically a vigorous man, but of delicate constitution."

Yet, stubbornly, he joined the army. Meanwhile, that term, "delicate constitution," plus reference to his small stature, keeps showing up in descriptions of him.

He first shows up in the US Army archives when he was commissioned as a second lieutenant in the 2nd Dragoon Regiment, on June 13, 1836, age twenty-one. He had no prior military experience, nor had he spent time at a government military academy, so he must have solicited a direct appointment. This was possible for a "young gentleman" with good references, and indicated that his family had the necessary connections.

Surviving army documents invariably use his middle initial rather than his middle name. The 1903 Historical Register[7] of US officers lists his name as Seth Barton Thornton, and at this writing the National Archives indexes his material under that name. However, the previously mentioned lawsuits over the management of his family's estate list his middle name as Brett, and the genealogical information later provided by his sister also gives it as Brett.

The formation of the 2nd Dragoons had been approved by Congress the previous month to deal specifically with the Indian troubles (subsequently known as the Second Seminole War) that had erupted in Florida. US negotiators had previously gotten the Seminoles to agree to move to what is now Arkansas to clear Florida for white settlers. However, on reconsideration, some of the Seminoles rebelled against the idea. Organized hostilities were under way by the end of 1835.

He was attached to Company D, which was immediately set up in Florida using recruits that had already arrived and would otherwise have gone to the 1st Dragoons. The rest of the regiments began organizing in sixty-man companies in boot camps in various cities, and did not begin appearing in Florida until late in the year. Why Thornton was sent straight to the front is not recorded, but it hints that there was no lack of confidence in him. Company D first saw action on July 19, 1836, at Welika Pond, near Fort Defiance (modern Micanopy in north-central Florida). The detachment, with sixty-four soldiers, fought off an attack on a wagon train, losing two dead and ten wounded. 2nd Lieutenant Thornton, however, was not specifically named as being there.[8]

He was, on the other hand, named as being at Fort Mellon (between modern Orlando and Daytona Beach) when it suffered a major assault on February 6, 1837, the Seminoles being driven off after three hours, leaving six soldiers wounded.[9]

In April 1837 he was made assistant commissary for subsistence[10] and was probably in the field less often. Then on November 16, 1837, he was promoted to first lieutenant.[11]

In early 1838 he was on the rolls of Fort Heilman, a depot in northeast Florida, twenty-five miles southwest of Jacksonville. Starting in May 1838 he was listed as being sick, and then on furlough, to Fort Monroe, Virginia, presumably meaning he was to report there after his furlough.[12] Newly completed, Fort Monroe protected the entrance to Chesapeake Bay.

During that period came the event that changed everything, forcing him to fight for his life and then his career.

The *Pulaski* was a packet steamer, meaning it carried passengers, their luggage, and mail, rather than bulk cargo. It was a side-wheeler, with an engine on each side. Intended for speed, it was lightly built. It would stop at Savannah and Charleston, and then head overnight to Baltimore.

She left Charleston on the morning of June 14, 1838, and headed into the Atlantic. About 11:00 p.m.—well after dark, and well out of sight of land—the starboard engine exploded. The wrecked hull bobbed on the surface for about forty minutes, taking on more and more water, and then collapsed, part sinking, the rest breaking into wooden debris rafts that quickly drifted apart. Two lifeboats managed to pull away while the other survivors clung to the debris in the darkness and pounding waves.

This was before radio or even telegraph connections, and the only realistic hope the survivors had was that another ship would happen to see them. The two lifeboats managed to make it to shore on an isolated beach northeast of Wilmington, North Carolina. But the news they brought spread at the speed of horseback riders, and there was no way to alert ships already at sea. Days went by, with storms and then relentless sun, and on the debris rafts the injured, the children, and the elderly died of exposure.

In the end, fifty-nine people were saved, and about 129 were lost.

Lieutenant Thornton was listed as one of the passengers who boarded in Charleston. A newspaper account written within days of the disaster mentions[13] thirteen survivors coming ashore, apparently on June 20, near the inlet of the New River, putting them in the vicinity of what is now Camp Lejeune, North Carolina. They were spread among a boat and several fragments of debris. The names of eleven of the thirteen were known and rendered as Samuel Bryley, Talbot County, Maryland; Owen Gallagher; Andrew Stevens, G. B. Lamar, G. Y. Yates, R. S. Hubbard, of New York; H. Eldridge, Syracuse, New York; Mr. Bennett of Missouri; Lt. Thornton, USA; B. W. Forsdick, Boston; and Mr. Merritt, Mobile.

On the other hand, an account[14] written by one of the survivors and published in 1919 mentions a small piece of wreckage washing ashore to which clung seven people: "Judge Rochester of New York, Mr. Baker of Georgia, two negro women and another scalded fireman, Lt. Thornton USA, and another gentleman."

The first scalded fireman (i.e., boiler tender) was put in one of the lifeboats and did not survive the trip to shore. There is no one named Baker on the passenger list, but he might have been a crewman. Judge Rochester, meanwhile, would be former US congressman, New York state judge, and ambassador to Colombia, William B. Rochester. He had apparently been returning to his home in Buffalo from tending to a business venture in Pensacola.

But while it's tempting to dwell on the possibility that Thornton tried to save a VIP, the Biographical Directory of the United States Congress says Judge Rochester was lost at sea, and doesn't mention him washing up anywhere.[15] And the contemporary newspaper account of the disaster has Judge Rochester in one of the lifeboats, drowning when it capsized in the surf within yards of dry land.

Obviously, the two accounts don't match. But that's hardly surprising—disasters breed chaos. Lieutenant Thornton himself probably didn't know the names of his fellow castaways.

About nine years later, in Mexico, he told a journalist that he saved his life by clinging to a chicken coop. "He picked several (passengers) out of the water, but one by one they died and dropped off, and he himself became a half-famished maniac before he was found. In military affairs he was always unfortunate. He was endowed with a courage that nothing could daunt; but his spirit was much too ardent and impetuous for his physical structure, he being of a small stature and a delicate constitution."[16]

Meanwhile, all the accounts of the disaster agree that the passenger list included Maj. G. L. Twiggs and his son, J. D. Twiggs. They were among thirty people picked up from a debris raft by a passing schooner, about twenty miles out to sea from the New River inlet, on the morning of the 19th, after five days in the water.

Maj. G. L. Twiggs was George Lowe Twiggs, born in 1789 near what is now Augusta, Georgia. (The military rank must have been from the local militia, since he is not listed as having been in US service.) His son, John David Twiggs, would have been about fifteen at the time.

But what's significant is that Maj. G. L. Twiggs was an older brother of Col. David E. Twiggs, commander of the 2nd Dragoons and therefore Lieutenant Thornton's commanding officer. (Meanwhile, Maj. G. L. Twiggs should not be confused with another of his younger brothers, Levi Twiggs, USMC, who was a major at the time of the Mexican-American War, but was a captain in 1838. To add to the confusion, Levi Twiggs also had a son, George Decatur Twiggs, who was about ten at the time of the disaster.[17])

There is no indication that Thornton had any hand in saving the lives of his commander's brother and nephew, or that they even saw each other after the explosion—it was night, and they ended up on widely separated debris rafts. On the other hand, they were listed next to each other among the passengers who boarded in Charleston, so they likely did interact before the explosion. But, clearly, he had a unique connection with his commander's family. That may explain how he managed to stay in the army for the next few years, despite his own maladroit actions.

George Lowe Twiggs's 1853 obituary noted that he never got over the *Pulaski* disaster. "Though of powerful frame and iron constitution, he had been for several years in failing health. He was one of the survivors on board the ill-fated *Pulaski*, wrecked in June 1838, and never entirely recovered from the effects of exposure for five days and five nights upon a portion of the wreck. In some degree the cause of the paralysis under which he suffered in his final illness can be traced to that memorable and appalling event."[18]

As for his son John David Twiggs, he apparently did recover, as he was later a lieutenant colonel in a Confederate cavalry unit. He was killed during the Civil War, but at the hands of his plantation overseer. The latter escaped punishment because the only witness was black, and at that time and place a white man could not be convicted on the testimony of a black man.[19]

As for Lieutenant Thornton, he clearly didn't get over it immediately either. While previously his delicate constitution had not kept him out of the field, after the disaster he was asking for light duty, and had to fight to stay in the army. That fight triggered a feud, which soon had a life of its own.

After June 1838 he was deskbound, on recruiting duty for more than a year, in Lancaster, Pennsylvania, and later in New Orleans, and finally Fort Columbus (modern Fort Jay, on Governor's Island in New York City's harbor). At Fort Columbus he was attached to the regiment's quartermaster company, in September 1839.

He does not reappear in the field until December 1839 when, as commander (as a senior lieutenant) of Company G, he founded Fort Virginia Braden,[20] the site of modern Fort Braden, a small town about fifteen miles west of modern Tallahassee. He was moved from that command in February and appears on the rolls of other forts in northern Florida through 1840, at one point being shown as acting quartermaster and commissary, indicating he was back at a desk job rather than in the field.

All this time, the question uppermost in his mind was what effect all those desk assignments would have on his chances for promotion. This becomes clear in a preserved letter[21] to Lieutenant Thornton from the adjutant general of the army, Bvt. Brig. Gen. Roger ap Catesby Jones,[22] dated August 28, 1840.

Your communication of the 10th instant, with sundry letters, including the certificate of doctors Foote and Moore, relative to the state of your health, have been duly received under cover of General Armistead's note of the same date. These papers are filed with the Joint Report of the Colonel and Major of your Regiment, of your being "physically unable to perform the duties of Captain of Dragoons" all of which will be duly weighed, when the time for your promotion comes around. In your letter of the 10th instant to General Armistead, you refer to your having been placed on the recruiting service, by my orders in the autumn of 1838—this is correct, but the official records, and my recollection of the case, establish the fact, that you were ordered on this service in consequence to the feeble state of your health, upon which indeed, you were unable to continue, as seen by my letter to you of the 19th of November 1838. (Vide your reports of September 24th, and November 2, 1838.)

I informed Colonel Twiggs of these facts (i.e., the reasons why you were temporarily put on the recruiting service) on the 26th of February, 1839.

It is due to candor, I should say to you, that, the very numerous reports you have from time to time have made to this office of your impaired constitution, have all along, impressed upon my mind the question of your promotion, long before the Report of your Colonel was received. But in communicating this impression of the question of expediency, you may rest assured, that whenever the time for your promotion may arrive the subject shall be duly weighed, and full justice be accorded to you and the service.

Gen. Walker K. Armistead was then commander of the army in Florida, and the reference to him indicates that Lieutenant Thornton went through proper channels. But the tone of the letter, discernible between the lines of exquisite wording, is that Thornton really should shut up. Snowing headquarters with letters and certificates was drawing attention to his problem rather than helping his case.

But what was this "Joint Report" the letter referred to? The colonel and major of his regiment told General Jones that he, Lieutenant Thornton, was "physically unable to perform the duties of Captain of Dragoons"? And the general had put the words in quotation marks, as if to show they were not his, and that he did not necessarily agree.

These fears came to the surface four months later, on December 23, at Fort Brooke, located at what is now downtown Tampa.[23] The 2nd Dragoons were passing through that day (six companies took part in a sweep of the Everglades, then in progress) and Thornton evidently had an administrative job at the fort. When the dragoons pitched camp, the head of the expedition, Maj. Thomas Turner Fauntleroy, demanded that Lieutenant Thornton, being a dragoon, move his tent into the dragoon camp.

Keep in mind that Major Fauntleroy was the major who submitted the mysterious Joint Report mentioned in General Jones's letter, questioning Thornton's fitness. He was, indeed, the only major in the regiment.

Fauntleroy, born in 1796 in Virginia, had been commissioned directly to the rank of major when the regiment was formed in 1836. Why, at age forty, he rated induction at the rank of major isn't clear. Perhaps he served as a teenager during the War of 1812,[24] although he is nowhere listed as having previously held a US military commission. In any event, it would take ten years, a declaration of war, and a massive expansion of the army before he got his first promotion.

That December day in 1840 the regimental adjutant, British native 2nd Lt. Robert G. Asheton was sent to fetch Capt. Croghan Ker to take part in a board of fitness. Lieutenant Asheton found Captain Ker in the tent that Lieutenant Thornton had just erected in the dragoon camp on orders from Major Fauntleroy.

The encounter was awkward. Thornton supposedly greeted him with the words, "God damn you, you damn puppy," and then made a noise with his mouth expressive of extreme contempt—as Asheton later complained. Thornton told Asheton to say what he had to say to Captain Ker and then get out, as "none but gentlemen" were allowed in his tent.

Lieutenant Thornton then went back to his old tent outside the dragoon encampment. Another lieutenant was sent to tell him that he was under arrest and to return to the dragoon camp, but he did not show up until the next morning.

And so the next day Major Fauntleroy apparently dropped everything else and put together a court-martial, and proceedings began that day, the 24th. Thornton was faced with three charges.

The first, conduct unbecoming an officer and a gentleman, stemmed from his alleged use of insulting and abusive language to Lieutenant Asheton while the latter was conducting official duties.

The second was disobedience of orders, as he did not "repair immediately to his tent" in the dragoon camp, when under arrest, when ordered to do so by Major Fauntleroy.

The third was breach of arrest, as he was gone that night, reappearing in the morning. He later moved his furniture to the new tent.

Only one member of the jury was from the dragoons, with the rest being pulled from an infantry regiment that was also at the fort. They were obviously unimpressed, asking how Thornton was supposed to be under arrest and move his tent at the same time.

Under questioning, Asheton admitted that he was not wearing his sword—the sign that the wearer was on duty and conducting official business—at the time of his encounter with Thornton. "They just get in the way," he said, noting that there were eleven dragoon officers in the camp, but only two had swords.

Captain Ker said Lieutenant Thornton told Lieutenant Asheton, "Go through with your duty," rather than "God damn you, you damn puppy." He was closer to Thornton than Asheton was, and was sure he heard it correctly. (The contemptuous noise wasn't addressed.)

After getting a postponement of several days, Lieutenant Thornton read a prepared statement—and came out swinging, barely acknowledging the official charges.

"The cause of my appearance before you cannot be seen from the charges and specifications," he said. "The circumstances are of too trivial a character to call for such proceedings. For causes unknown to me I have long been the object of the bitter persecution of the first and third officers in rank in the regiment. Asheton has been a willing instrument."

He said they were apparently trying to get rid of him, and mentioned the Joint Report that General Jones referred to, calling it a secret letter since it was never shown to him. He complained that the letter suggested that the next person in rank (after Lieutenant Thornton) be promoted to the next vacancy, yet no medical board had been convened and no medical opinions had been sought.

"Lt. Asheton was used as the instrument, as he has mentioned more than once the subject of my being overslaughed with great apparent satisfaction, and in one instance informed one of my juniors of his fair prospects of rapid promotion as I would not fill the next vacancy," he added—and then announced that Lieutenant Asheton was a deserter from the British army.

The court then deliberated and pronounced its findings: guilty on the charge of conduct unbecoming an officer and a gentleman, and not guilty of disobedience of orders and breach of arrest. Lieutenant Thornton was sentenced to be "admonished of the impropriety of his conduct."

In other words, they shrugged off two of the three charges, and for the third Thornton barely got a slap on the wrist. The look on Major Fauntleroy's face must have been priceless.

On the outside of the case file is the notation, "Respectfully laid before the general-in-chief, does not the accusation herein alleged against the adjutant demand consideration and investigation?"

Perhaps it did—Asheton is listed as being dismissed from the service six months later, on June 22, 1841, a little over a month after he suddenly disappeared.[25]

Meanwhile, on February 1, 1841, the question of Lieutenant Thornton's promotion was finally settled, and he was elevated to captain.[26] The promotion raised his pay from $33.33 to $50 per month, plus he got an extra $10 per month when in command of a company. (The extra money was in recognition of the fact that the captain of a company was, under section 40 of the Articles of War, accountable for the loss, spoilage, or damage of the "arms, clothing, or other warlike stores" of the company except from unavoidable damages or actual service.) Plus he was entitled to four rations per day, plus forage for two horses and pay for one servant, all of which were the same perks a lieutenant received. A ration was food for one day (not one meal, as in modern usage) and for officers was figured at 20 cents per ration, so he could count on an extra 80 cents per day. Forage was $8 per month for each horse the officer actually owned and kept in service. The servant got the pay of a private, which was $8 per month in the dragoons, plus one ration and a monthly clothing allowance of $2.50, but the servant had to be actually in service. (Pay was slightly less in the infantry and artillery: $40 for a captain, $30 for a lieutenant, and $7 for a private. The number of servants allowed was the same, but you had to be a major or above to get forage.[27]) (By comparison, agricultural laborers got about a dollar a day, blacksmiths, machinists and carpenters about $1.25, while a skilled shovel-maker might get $2 per day.[28])

But after all the anxiety, how did Captain Thornton suddenly prevail? Perhaps General Jones was true to his promise to "do justice." Perhaps Colonel Twiggs relented, for whatever reason. Perhaps he relented because of the never-mentioned connection of the *Pulaski* disaster. Or, facing an officer shortage, headquarters simply preferred not to throw any away.

But events were to show that Major Fauntleroy had not relented, and that Captain Thornton had learned nothing nor forgotten anything—those two were not through with each other.

After his promotion, Captain Thornton appears on the rolls of various forts across Florida for the next year.

During 1841 it was decided to launch a summer offensive, something the US Army had justifiably avoided doing in Florida, fearing the heat would be worse than the Indians. In June they sent a force of about four hundred, mostly infantry, against the band of a chieftain named Halleck-Tustenugge in the vicinity of Fort King (modern Ocala) in central Florida. He had perhaps thirty-five followers, but odds of ten to one were considered optimal for stalking Seminoles. He was encamped on some dry land where the attackers hoped to surprise him at dawn after wading through six miles of swamp in moonless darkness.

A memoirist among the infantry later described how the silence (such as it was) during this ordeal was broken by none other than Capt. Seth Thornton giving another display of stubbornness. After the column had spent hours floundering single-file through the darkness, Capt. Thornton unexpectedly turned out to be the person in line behind the memoirist.

"Who is that in advance?" inquired Seth Thornton, in a whisper.

"Lee," was a whisper reply.

"Give us your arm, old fel. I am a fallen swamp-angel, weak in the knees, and damned near dead. Hold on to me while I drink like a horse."

Poor Seth! He had a lion's heart, but no physical ability. The colonel had in kindness ordered him to remain back in the pines with the (wagon) train, finding that persuasion was a no avail; but, orders or no orders, if there was any fighting to be done, Seth Thornton wouldn't be scarce.

We all know that how he battled with disease to the last and died, as he wished to die, a soldier's death on the plains of Mexico.

"Lincoln, is that you?"

This interrogation was prompted by an unchristian exclamation of "Damn!" in our immediate vicinity in deep water.

"Yes. Where the hell is the trail, and who are you?"

"Friend, with the countersign."

"All right, Lee. Advance and take something. Who is with you?"

"Seth."

"Seth Thornton? Why, Thornton, I told you that you were a fool to attempt this expedition. Your heart is too big for legs; you have the legs of a coot."

"Fool! Coot!" exclaimed Seth. "I will hold you responsible for this language, sir, tomorrow."

Poor Seth's head was carried off by an 18-pound ball in the advance on the City of Mexico, so he had no chance for last dying words; but had he died with the death rattle in his throat, there is no doubt that in his last utterances he would have been holding someone responsible for something "tomorrow."[29]

(A coot is a water bird with skinny legs. The names and expletives were obscured with dashes in the original but could be surmised.)

Of course, when they arrived, the Seminoles weren't there. The army had more luck during other missions, but by the end of the summer about one man in six of the field force had been hospitalized. Also during that summer Capt. Thornton became commander of Company F, entitling him to that extra $10 per month.

With the coming of winter he was back in the swamp again, as his company was one of two involved in a sweep of Big Cypress Swamp on the north side of the Everglades. The sweep lasted from November 1, 1941, to February 7, 1842, driving out the hostiles but triggering no fighting.[30] He was back at Fort Braden with his company in April 1842.

About that time the authorities decided to end the Second Seminole War by, basically, declaring victory and getting out. Amid the fruitless search-and-destroy missions, small boat expeditions, scouting sweeps, road patrols, and wagon escorts, there had been moments of terror, and the regiment had lost more than fifty men in combat. At Tampa's Camp Brooke the dragoons kept an Irish wolfhound named Romeo who had been found at the site of a trading post where the Seminoles had killed eighteen people. When the site was reached two weeks later, the soldiers found that all the bodies had been dismembered by scavengers except one, guarded by that dog.[31]

As part of the retrenchment and re-orientation that followed the pull-out from Florida, on August 12, 1842, Captain Thornton and

Company F joined the post at Fort Jesup in west-central Louisiana, about twenty-two miles west of Natchitoches, accessible by Red River steamboats.

The fort was established in 1822 to watch the Sabine River, then the national border, during the Mexican Revolution and later the Texas Revolution. In 1842 the Sabine was still the national border, but with the Republic of Texas, then still embroiled in hostilities with Mexico. By then it had become a comfortable facility, with handsome quarters for both officers and men, a spacious parade and drill ground, a theater, a gymnasium, a school, a chapel, a library, and a retail store.

Eventually seven companies of the 2nd Dragoons were located at the fort. The other three companies were located at forts in what is now southeast Oklahoma to protect the settlers there from Plains Indians. (The settlers were themselves relocated Indians.)

At Fort Jesup they began an active training program inspired by Capt. William J. Hardee. He was one of three officers who had recently been sent to a one-year term at the École Royale de Cavalerie de Saumur (the French Army cavalry school in Saumur, France), graduating January 28, 1842. Bringing with him the woman he'd married just before leaving for France, he took up residence at the post in August, about the time Captain Thornton arrived. He led selected detachments through new drills, and experiments with lances and different swords, for instance.[32]

The post had a social life. Thornton's sister later recalled that a certain young lady visited the fort, "and in the exuberance of her youth and gaiety often subjected herself to unkind comment." During an officers' dinner party her name was "lightly given" in a toast. But Thornton rose and asked that the toast not be drunk, as "he occasionally visited the lady and could not listen to her name being lightly used." They backed off. (Apparently they had not adopted the British Army practice of banning any mention of women, religion, politics, or professional matters when officers dined.)

But then disaster struck from Washington. First was the retrenchment that cut the size of the companies. For dragoons, Congress set the number of non-officers to four sergeants, four corporals, two buglers, one farrier and blacksmith, and fifty privates. (A farrier is a specialist in the shoeing of horses. The blacksmith made the horseshoes.) Then, they decided the government didn't need to be feeding so many horses, so they converted the 2nd Dragoons into a rifle regiment, retaining their uniforms, and keeping the same organization with fifty privates per company, but dropping the farriers and blacksmiths. The horses were to be handed over to the 1st Dragoons, or sold.

On March 5, 1843, they officially became the dismounted 2nd Regiment of Riflemen—and lobbying was already under way to reverse the decision. The secretary of war reported that the monetary savings resulting from the conversion was not significant, and that the army's presumptive enemies (hostile Plains Indians) were mounted, and so mounted forces were required to counter them. One regiment of dragoons was not enough. The legislatures of Louisiana and Missouri also petitioned for a reversal.

So on March 4, 1844, they were again designated the 2nd Regiment of Dragoons, and were mounted again.

But having his command dismounted was not the biggest thing that happened to Captain Thornton in the spring of 1843. Instead, his old nemesis Major Fauntleroy showed up at the fort, and Thornton immediately clashed with him. As a result he was nearly thrown out of the army.

In fact, he probably should have been thrown out, as the facts show that he tried to provoke a duel with a superior officer. Someone proved willing to overlook that.

Still commanding Company F, he went on leave from January 9 to March 15, 1843, and so missed the dismounting process.[33] Then, on April 13, Major Fauntleroy showed up at the fort. He'd been with the regiment's detachments in Oklahoma where, presumably, they didn't need newly dismounted dragoons.

On April 15 Colonel Twiggs issued a general order putting Major Fauntleroy in charge of the fort's police, roll calls, inspections, etc.[34] But earlier that day, in the post reading room, in front of witnesses, after ascertaining that Major Fauntleroy was not on duty, Captain Thornton confronted him.

"Major Fauntleroy, in consequence of your course towards me, I brand you as a liar and assassin," witnesses recalled him saying.

Major Fauntleroy replied, lawyer-like, "I suppose this is on account of my official course towards you, in reporting you at Washington." Thornton agreed—which was unwise, because Major Fauntleroy slipped the word "official" in there, cloaking his letter-writing as official duty.

The upshot was that Thornton was put under arrest, relieved of his command, and charged with three offenses: expressing disrespect of a superior officer for what he said on the 15th to Major Fauntleroy's face; conduct unbecoming an officer and a gentleman for what he did on the 15th and for saying something similar about the major in front of witnesses on the 14th; and mutinous conduct, for what he did on the 15th.

The charges did not cite violations of the Articles of War, which was the US law code governing the military at the time. But Article 7 said that the punishment for mutiny was, "death, or such other punishment as by the court martial shall be inflicted." Under Article 5, the punishment for expressing disrespect was to be cashiered (thrown out of the army) "or other punishment as the court martial shall direct." Under Article 83, the punishment for "conduct unbecoming an officer and a gentleman" was to be dismissed from the service. So the stakes were high.

It would not have been Captain Thornton's only flirtation with dueling, despite the severe penalties. His sister said he was once in New Orleans walking down the street with another (unnamed) officer, when someone walking the other direction insulted the other officer, who pretended not to notice. When Thornton later asked him what that was all about, the other officer said that man had been trying to provoke him into a duel, but as family man he would not take the risk. Back at his hotel, Thornton wrote to the provocateur, saying that he shared the insult with the other officer by position and so was demanding an apology—and that he himself had no reservations about fighting a duel. The recipient backed down.

The trial convened on May 29, 1843, at Fort Jesup. Captain Thornton pled not guilty to all the charges.

Proceedings began, oddly, with Major Fauntleroy demanding that one of the members of the court, Capt. R. L. Dix, be dismissed, as the man was "personally hostile to him and therefore prejudiced against him."

After clearing the court and deliberating, the members refused to sustain the objection.

And that set for tone for the rest of the proceedings, as nearly every time Thornton posed a question Fauntleroy would object to it—and be overruled. However, his objections usually seemed sound, as the intent of many of Thornton's questions was to bring up the history between himself and Fauntleroy, rather than address the specific charges against him.

Curiously, Captain Dix was then called as the first witness for the prosecution, and recalled Thornton denouncing Fauntleroy on the 14th. As an aside, he mentioned that it happened moments after Thornton was asked to vacate his quarters so that Fauntleroy could occupy the entire building. (This apparent provocation wasn't addressed further.) Another officer also recalled witnessing the denunciation.

Then Colonel Twiggs himself was called. He said he knew nothing about what had gone on between Thornton and Fauntleroy. That should have been the end of his testimony—but then Thornton began asking him about that 1840 letter to the adjutant general. The questioning continued despite Fauntleroy's constant, unsuccessful objections.

Yes, the colonel said, there had been such a letter, saying Lieutenant Thornton was physically incapable and should not be promoted, written some time in 1840, signed by Major Fauntleroy, and sent to the adjutant general. But it was official correspondence and there was nothing secret about it, although no copy of it was kept in the regiment's office. "It was given to the adjutant and I thought it was copied," Twiggs testified. "But I found on examination that it was not. The adjutant was told distinctly that there was no secret about it."

The adjutant, of course, was Lieutenant Asheton, who had since deserted.

Colonel Twiggs also recalled Major Fauntleroy asking if a copy of the letter ought to be sent to Lieutenant Thornton, but he (Twiggs) thought it was not necessary. He does not explain, nor does anyone ask, how he could possibly have thought that. But even the original regimental historian described him as "arbitrary and capricious," ruling with an iron hand.[35]

Fauntleroy then asked Twiggs, "Did I not expressly declare my desire at the time that the letter was written not to impeach Lt. Thornton's honor in any manner whatever and that my concurrence in the letter was under an imperious sense of duty, which you thought to exist with the field officers of the regiment, in the absence of an inspector general?"

"There was a great deal of conversation relative to the matter," Twiggs replied. "I cannot recollect all that was said; it was distinctly understood between us that we were to confine ourselves to the single fact of his physical capacity. As there had been no inspector general to the regiment while serving in the field since its formation a report should be made to the Adjutant General."

There was further testimony from other witnesses about the events of April 15th, and then the prosecution rested.

Then Thornton launched his defense—and did not mention the actual charges. Instead he called six different officers to ask them if they had heard about the letter. All had, and most thought it was some kind of secret.

Then he veered even further off topic and called Capt. T. B. Linnard, a topographical engineer. "Did you state to me on or about the fourth of February 1843 that you felt sure that you had heard Major Fauntleroy express his willingness to give personal satisfaction to any officer who felt injured by his military conduct?"

This was explosive. "To give satisfaction" meant to fight a duel. Of the 101 sections of the Articles of War, four dealt directly with the suppression of dueling. The punishment for issuing a challenge to a duel (much less fighting one) was dismissal from the army. To allow someone else to fight a duel, to cooperate with arranging one, or to rebuke someone for not accepting a challenge, invoked the same punishment. Basically, duels were forbidden, and everyone was supposed to take part in suppressing them or get out of the army.

Not surprisingly, there was an objection to the question, and Thornton withdrew it while he composed a justification for offering it. Meanwhile, the court adjourned until the next day.

When they reconvened the next day, Thornton explained that the question was necessary for his defense since he (Thornton) may have viewed the declaration by Major Fauntleroy of his willingness to provide satisfaction as an invitation to demand it, or provoke a meeting which Thornton could not decline. "He would have been influenced by this consideration when he sought an interview (on April 15) with Major Fauntleroy, believing Major Fauntleroy was not on duty." Also, "Although the provocation given by Major Fauntleroy might not fully justify, it might mitigate."

In other words, he admitted he was trying to challenge Major Fauntleroy to a duel, or accept a challenge that he believed Fauntleroy had already issued. Either would be a serious violation of the Articles of War. But the fact that he could show he had been provoked mitigated his guilt under the charges—or so he argued.

The court members remained sympathetic, and voted to allow him to pose the question to Captain Linnard.

Linnard answered that he felt sure—but was not absolutely certain—that he had heard Major Fauntleroy say such a thing, "last spring on a steamboat near the Red River Raft."

Thornton then submitted supporting documents, including the August 29, 1840, letter from the adjutant general that mentioned the letter questioning his capacity, and also the doctor's certificates. Then, after another postponement, he submitted his closing argument.

He argued that he did not express disrespect for a superior officer on April 14 and 15 since Major Fauntleroy was not on duty at the time. His own actions were explained by the provocation of the secret letter, written when he was on active duty in the field, and having no foundation in truth. "I believe it to have been a secret and malicious attempt to drive me out of the army," he said, adding that he didn't think that a court-martial against Major Fauntleroy would produce much result, as the major would just plead duty, saying he had written the letter for the good of the service.

"It only remained for me to await a proper occasion to seek redress in the manner usual among gentleman of all professions. . . . You cannot attach blame to me for resenting what I believed to be an insult of the most aggravated character."

After hearing Major Fauntleroy's summation (illegible in the surviving file), the court deliberated and then gave its verdict: guilty on all counts. They sentenced Captain Thornton to be reprimanded in orders and suspended without pay for five months.

It was another slap on the wrist, considering that he was clearly guilty not only of the charges but of trying to challenge a superior officer to a duel—to kill him in a socially acceptable manner, in other words. On June 8 General Arbuckle issued General Order 23 from military district headquarters in New Orleans, summarizing the charges and outcome of the trial. The general approved the proceedings and findings of the court, and, "as a matter of duty confirms the sentence and directs that it be carried into execution."

"It cannot be hoped that the discipline of the army can be maintained when the courts award punishment so inadequate to the offences committed," the order continued. Even if Major Fauntleroy offered satisfaction, "It could in no way justify the conduct of Capt. Thornton, who is amply protected by the laws of his country from the oppression or injustice of superiors."

But it is clear that the focus of Captain Thornton's paranoia had changed since December 1840, and he no longer included Colonel Twiggs as an oppressor. Presumably, he mellowed when he actually got the promotion that the letter tried to deny him, and which Twiggs could have blocked. Instead, he now saw Major Fauntleroy as a personal enemy but held no enmity against Twiggs, calling him as a friendly witness. Nor did Twiggs have anything negative to say about him at the trial.

Curiously, none of the surviving documents address the exact nature of Thornton's incapacity. His sister mentioned that his health gave him problems when he was in school, but after entering the army it did not stop him from being active in the field. There was no hint of incapacity prior to the *Pulaski* disaster in June 1838. The aftermath of that incident forced him to take desk jobs for a while, and his infirmity was obvious enough to trigger a letter to the adjutant general in 1840, but did not prevent his promotion in early 1841, or prevent him from commanding a company thereafter. He returned from suspension and resumed command of Company F on November 25, 1843, and remained there until the next summer. In the meantime the regiment reconverted to dragoons, the re-designation becoming official on March 5, 1844.

Then, on August 8, 1844, Captain Thornton relinquished command of Company F and went on sick leave, and then a leave of absence, not returning to the fort (and resuming command of Company F) until June 17, 1845.[36]

He was just in time for the war brewing with Mexico—a war he would start.

CHAPTER 3

Advance to Contact

THE UNITED STATES AND MEXICO HAD BEEN DRIFTING TOWARD WAR ever since the Mexican government refused to recognize the secession and independence of Texas in 1836. Mexican public opinion also widely assumed that the Texan rebels were puppets of the US government. Certainly the rebellious Texans were almost entirely former US residents, who could count on the sympathy of the US government and public, especially after Mexican dictator (and on-and-off general) Antonio López de Santa Anna tried to suppress the rebellion with well-publicized massacres.

He failed miserably, and was taken prisoner by the Texan rebels after the detachment of the Mexican army he was leading was destroyed at the Battle of San Jacinto (April 21, 1836) near modern Houston. (After cornering the Texan army he inexplicably decided to take a siesta and let his army do the same. Then, the Texans attacked.) In captivity he signed the so-called Treaty of Velasco, recognizing Texas independence and setting the border on the Rio Grande.

The Mexican government disavowed both the treaty and Santa Anna, and pursued a border war with Texas until a truce in 1843. But Santa Anna would not let the matter rest, treating his personal humiliation as a national humiliation. During his 1841–1844 restoration Santa Anna had erected a bronze statue of himself in front of the National Theater in Mexico City. He was depicted mounted on a horse, pointing north, toward Texas, to remind Mexicans of the need to retake Texas. (It was also pointing toward the mint, wits invariably noted.)

Actual annexation of Texas by the US was delayed by politics, since slavery was legal in the Republic of Texas, and so adding Texas as a state would increase the number of slave states and their power in the US Congress. The necessary legislation finally passed in March 1845, although several ratification steps were still required before annexation was final.

The Mexican government was outraged and severed ties with the United States. However, the newly elected US president, James Knox Polk, assumed something could be worked out—especially if he applied what he called "graduated pressure" to the Mexican government.

Complicating the situation was the fact that the US legislation admitting Texas did not define its territory. Provisional recognition offered by Mexico at the same time (the abortive Cuevas-Smith Treaty, which required that Texas stay out of the United States) didn't either. But by annexing Texas the US government tacitly inherited Texas's claim that its southern border was the Rio Grande. The Mexican government insisted the border was the old provincial boundary, mostly running along the Rio Nueces, as much as 200 miles to the north. The intervening Trans-Nueces Region (also known as the Nueces Strip, or the Wild Horse Desert) was a largely uninhibited wasteland of interest to neither government. The Mexican army had retreated south of the Rio Grande, and the Republic of Texas had done little to administer the region. But the Rio Grande stretched all the way to the Rocky Mountains, and using it as a border could turn Texas from a provincial spin-off into an empire.

But the two countries might still have gone to war had Texas not existed, since there was another major issue that also would not go away. Mexican military units often funded themselves by expropriations, i.e., taking what they needed at gunpoint. Mexican citizens could regard their losses as investments in local political influence, but foreigners had no such comfort. They could, however, get their governments to help them press claims against the Mexican government to recover their losses, turning expropriations into international incidents. US citizens had been increasingly doing that. Some had been shaken down for cash, others had lost whole ships, cargoes, or both. Sometimes there had been a flimsy legal pretext, and other times there were no such frills. US diplomats were making more and more trouble about the claims, especially as no restitution was ever forthcoming.

President Andrew Jackson, in his February 6, 1837, message to Congress, made it sound like war was being seriously considered. The nature of the claims against Mexico and the way they have been handled "would justify, in the eyes of all nations, immediate war. That remedy, however, should not be used by just and generous nations, confiding in their strength, for injuries committed, if it can be honorably avoided," he said.[1]

French citizens had also been victimized, and a few months later, in 1838, France blockaded the Gulf Coast of Mexico and seized control of the port of Vera Cruz, officially to collect damages of $600,000 claimed by its citizens. (Santa Anna lost his left leg while fighting a French landing party during the affair, called the Pastry War. This served to rehabilitate him from the shame of losing Texas two years earlier.)

In 1839 the United States and Mexico set up a commission to examine the claims of US citizens. By the time its term expired in February 1842, despite constant foot-dragging by the Mexican members, the commission had awarded claims of $2,026,139.68. They were never paid. Claims awarded by the American commissioners but not adjudicated by the Mexican commissioners amounted to another $928,027.88. Submitted claims that the commission had not had time to examine before dissolving totaled $3,336,837.05. The Mexican government never convened a new commission to examine the additional claims, as originally agreed.[2]

With claims at least five times that of the French (ten times if the additional claims are included) a US move similar to the one the French took in 1838 looked inevitable. For the sake of scale, $6 million would have been enough to cover US defense spending for more than six months.

Meanwhile, as the annexation crisis escalated, Santa Anna was sitting it out in Cuba, having gone into exile after being deposed in late 1844. While he was known to occasionally engineer his own removal by one junta or another after he got bored or saw that the government was about to run out of money, this time it was real. This time he'd alienated too many backers with his extravagances—and by the way he kept raising taxes to pay for them. He asked for $4 million to re-conquer Texas, and when the Mexican Congress agreed, he raised the ante to $10 million. They balked. Marrying (at age fifty) a fifteen-year-old girl forty-one days after the death of his first wife was the final straw for many. Rioters tore down his statue and desecrated the grave where his left leg had been ceremoniously interred. He fled after a brief civil war, and former minister of war José Joaquín de Herrera became the new president.[3]

With the Texans becoming US citizens and entitled to the protection of the US Army, another reorientation was in order, and Washington concentrated two infantry regiments (the 3rd and 4th) at Fort Jesup, as well as seven companies of the 2nd Dragoons.

In mid-June, after the Texas Congress had ratified annexation, the force at Fort Jesup was sent to occupy the coastal hamlet of Corpus Christi, which had been serving as a trading post for smugglers undercutting the Mexican government's monopoly on tobacco.[4] Located just south of the Rio Nueces outlet on the Gulf of Mexico, it was within the disputed Trans-Nueces Region—albeit just barely. From that point the US Army could exert another level of graduated pressure, while being out of reach of any sudden sortie by a Mexican force. Indeed, the Trans-Nueces wasteland itself amounted to a fortification, since the local Mexican army did not have a supply train to get across it.

The infantry traveled by ships from New Orleans, but the dragoons marched overland through Texas. It was a show of force to reassure the Texans, but walking was also assumed to be better for the horses.[5] The three-company detachment in Oklahoma traveled separately to the Austin area, to guard the frontier.

The seven companies at Fort Jesup (which included Captain Thornton and Company F) marched on July 25, 1845, with about five hundred men and sixty supply wagons. They sortied well before dawn each morning (sometimes at midnight, if there was moonlight) to avoid the heat of the day.

As they passed Crockett, Texas, on August 4, the feud with Major Fauntleroy surfaced again.[6] As he testified later, Thornton was in the rear of a wagon at the rear of his company when Fauntleroy drove up to him in a buggy and told him to halt his company and let other wagons pass.

Thornton replied that there were three companies ahead of this one, so that if he did pass this company there'd still be others in the way. Fauntleroy repeated the order, so Thornton just rode ahead without replying.

He reached the head of his company and led the wagons about two hundred yards farther down the road to a clearing where they could drive off the road and stop.

Of course, had he obeyed Major Fauntleroy literally and halted his company in the road, they would have blocked the road with their wagons and no other wagons could have passed. Fauntleroy did not see it that way, and rode up and said so.

"Captain Thornton, you have disobeyed my orders," he yelled. "I ordered you to halt your company." He then rode off to see Colonel Twiggs, and got Thornton put under arrest. He remained under arrest until the 21st, when Fauntleroy thought to ask that he be released.

The unit reached Corpus Christi on August 27, having covered (according to their odometer) 501.5 miles, while spending eight days on the way resting. At Corpus Christi other units had already arrived by sea. The dragoons became concerned as they neared the coast when they thought they heard heavy cannon fire, but it turned out to be a tropical storm.

The next day, August 28, 1845, Captain Thornton asked for a court of inquiry to look into the reason for his arrest. His request was granted and proceedings began September 6.

Thornton submitted a brief going back over his history with Major Fauntleroy. He stated that the major's charge of disobedience came from "the settled purpose, which he has pursued for years, to deprive me of my commission. This hostility to me evinced itself as long ago as 1839 when he signed a letter to the adjutant general of the army impugning my 'physical inability' to perform the duties of my present rank and advising that a junior should be promoted over my head. . . . In one case he delayed the movement of his command into the field in order to prosecute charges against me, which resulted in my acquittal." The latter reference, of course, is to the December 1840 court-martial in Tampa.

Fauntleroy testified that he asked Thornton to pull over to let Capt. Charles May and his company pass, having heard from Captain May that it was his turn to be at the front of the column that day.

Captain May (like Captain Thornton, and for that matter Major Fauntleroy and Colonel Twiggs) was a founding member of the regiment, but had gotten his original second lieutenant's commission because his hometown was Washington, DC, and President Andrew Jackson had seen him there doing trick riding.[7] (This probably did not include an incident where he rode his horse both up and down the stairs of a hotel.) If the other members were dubious about the nature of his qualifications, they kept quiet about it after he served creditably in Florida.

When Thornton replied about other companies being ahead of his in the column, Fauntleroy said he thought Thornton wanted to argue because he was afraid of losing his place in the column. Fauntleroy said he followed in the rear of the company for a while after Thornton rode forward, and when they did not pull over he rode ahead and told the riders and wagons he encountered to pull over, which they did. When he got to the front he found Thornton getting the front of the column off the road, and there was a heated exchange about there having been no room to get off the road earlier. He does not, in the end, accuse Thornton of disobeying orders, but of using improper language and having a heated manner.

Finally, Colonel Twiggs testified that if the company whose turn it was to be first was not ready to march when the bugle sounded, those that were ready were supposed to march anyway, implying that sympathy for Captain May's problem was misplaced.

The court issued its findings on Friday, September 12, 1845: The orders of Major Fauntleroy had been duly obeyed and there had been no cause for the arrest of Captain Thornton.

So Thornton won again. Meanwhile his nemesis would no longer trouble him, as Fauntleroy was sent to the Austin area with the regiment's other three companies to watch the Indian frontier.

He would, however, end up troubling General Taylor. The general reported to Washington on November 19 that on October 30 Major Fauntleroy had raided an Indian camp outside Austin because a self-styled Texas "Indian agent" said they had been involved in depredations in the Corpus Christi area. Taylor (himself in the Corpus Christi area) knew of no such depredations, and Fauntleroy acted without inquiring further, he complained. Eight Comanches had surrendered without incident—but then tried to escape and two were shot.

"This circumstance is greatly to be regretted, and may be the germ of serious difficulty on the Indian frontier," Taylor wrote. "My instructions to Major Fauntleroy have been very pointed—to exercise great caution in all matters relating to alleged Indian depredations. . . . I shall give such instructions to Major Fauntleroy as will prevent a recurrence of such hasty and ill-judged proceedings hereafter."

By the time Major Fauntleroy was embarrassing both himself and his commander, General Taylor's force had risen to nearly four thousand soldiers as other units arrived. He organized it into three brigades, in addition to army-level troops that reported directly to him:[8]

- 1st Brigade, composed of the 8th Infantry Regiment, plus the Artillery Battalion (trained artillerymen acting as infantry).

- 2nd Brigade, composed of the 5th and 7th Infantry Regiments.

- 3rd Brigade, composed of the 3rd and 4th Infantry Regiments from Fort Jesup.

- Army-level troops: the 2nd Dragoon Regiment, three batteries of field artillery, and a platoon-size company of Texas Rangers.

While, as mentioned, the regiment was the basic administrative military unit at the time, the brigade was the basic maneuver unit, meaning that generals usually fought battles using brigades. (If a brigade became depleted, they would add more regiments.) Having three, as General Taylor did, was good practice, since there could be two on the line and one in reserve. Batteries, meanwhile, were the basic artillery unit, of four to six guns. It was the largest concentration that the US Army had fielded since the War of 1812. It also used up all but four regiments of the US Army: one was left to watch the entire Canadian border, and three to watch the Indians.

But the unit designations were almost silly as the US Congress's 1842 retrenchment was still in force, and most units were no more than 40 percent strength. They were called regiments, but were really battalions (a unit intermediate between a company and a regiment) as admitted by the designation of the Artillery Battalion. In the Napoleonic wars in Europe thirty years earlier, or the US Civil War fifteen years later, a force the size of the Army of Observation might have been considered sufficient to defend a specific hill. The mass armies in those conflicts often maneuvered as corps, defined as a formation that could break camp, march down a road, and make a new camp in the course of a day. That usually amounted to about twenty thousand men and their equipment, moving about sixteen miles. Corps were divided into divisions, and divisions into brigades, and brigades into regiments. (Today the division is often the basic all-arms maneuver unit.)

Meanwhile, in December 1845 President Polk decided that it was time to add diplomatic pressure to the military pressure presumably exerted by the presence of General Taylor's army. Mexico's President Herrera had indicated a willingness to talk, so Polk sent an emissary, John Slidell. He carried an offer to cover the $3 million in adjudicated US expropriation claims if Mexico would acknowledge the loss of Texas and sign over the Trans-Nueces. Beyond that, Polk offered as much as $25 million for the rest of northern Mexico, especially California and everything between it and Texas.

The United States could readily raise the money, as President Jackson had made a point of paying off the national debt through surplus land sales, giving the United States one day in its history (January 8, 1835) when it had no debt. It resumed accruing the next day, but it was a bookkeeping entry rather than an economic factor.

Total revenue for the debt-mired Mexican government had been $20.6 million in 1844, its best year to that time (versus expenses of $31.3 million[9]). Surely the money would be irresistible. What could go wrong?

But as Slidell arrived in Mexico his intention to buy huge (albeit lightly populated) swathes of Mexico became known, and the Mexican press and political classes went ballistic—who put up a for-sale sign? Herrera did not dare receive him. Herrera, to boost his own damaged credibility, then ordered Gen. Mariano Paredes in San Luis Potosi to march north to the border. (Paredes had been instrumental in helping Herrera overthrow Santa Anna and send him into exile.) Paredes had eight thousand soldiers—enough to stop, if not crush Taylor's army.

And march he did—south, to Mexico City, where he installed himself as president. Herrera resigned as president on December 30, 1845.[10]

President Polk reacted to the failure of graduated pressure by deciding that more pressure was needed. So on January 13, 1846, he sent word to General Taylor to advance his army to the Rio Grande, about 160 miles to the south. Taylor waited for better weather to start, and began moving March 8.

Meanwhile, Polk was approached by an emissary of Santa Anna, still in exile in Cuba. The deposed dictator expressed his love for peace and said that the Mexican government would probably be open to a settlement in exchange for $35 million (i.e., enough to float it for a year) especially if he himself were running things again. But to satisfy Mexican public opinion the agreement would have to look coerced. An invasion of northern Mexico and a blockade of Vera Cruz might be advisable.[11] In other words, graduated pressure, backed by a huge amount of money, was correct. It must have been exactly what Polk wanted to hear. And Santa Anna doubtless knew that.

Back at Corpus Christi, the dragoons and then each brigade marched one day apart, to give the watering holes time to recover. General Taylor had 3,550 soldiers, and a supply train of 307 wagons that must have by itself stretched three miles. The wagons carried twenty days' food for the men and sixteen days' food for the animals, which included about nine hundred horses, one thousand mules, and six hundred oxen.[12] They were to be resupplied through the Mexican port at Point Isabel (modern Port Isabel, Texas), north of Matamoros, after the US Navy seized it.

They encountered an outpost of Mexican cavalry March 19 at Arroyo Colorado, a slough about thirty miles north of Matamoros. They nervously crossed with two brigades the next day, but encountered no opposition. They proceeded south in four columns, rather than one long road column.

On March 24 the force reached a road junction about ten miles west of Point Isabel, which the US Navy was scheduled to seize that very day. Taylor rushed to the port with all seven companies of the 2nd Dragoons, leaving the rest of his force to head south to the watering hole at Palo Alto. He found that the landing had taken place about three hours earlier, but the retreating Mexican force had set some of the buildings on fire. Taylor had the place garrisoned and started construction of fortifications, and rejoined the main body, with the dragoons, on the 27th. His army was on the banks of the Rio Grande opposite Matamoros by noon the next day.

They camped in a duly leased farm field and began building the previously described fort, from which their artillery could demolish downtown Matamoros a mile away. Matamoros had a garrison of about three thousand soldiers. But except at bushwhackers and deserters, there was no shooting. The US side wanted to finish the fort, and as mentioned there was a power vacuum on the Mexican side, as the local commander, Gen. Mariano Arista, had not supported the latest coup in Mexico City.

His replacement arrived on April 11 with enough reinforcements (taken from San Luis Potosi) to bring the garrison up to fifty-two hundred men. But the replacement turned out to be Gen. Pedro de Ampudia. Either because of his actions during his previous tenure as a commander in the area, or because of his behavior in Tabasco two years earlier (see Chapter 5), he was positively loathed by powerful locals who demanded that he be replaced.

Needing the full support of the border population, the new junta agreed to restore General Arista. However, they left General Ampudia as second in command, apparently unaware that the two hated and distrusted each other. Until his replacement returned, Ampudia was told to suspend operations.[13] Grudgingly, he agreed.

Arista returned and on April 23 rendezvoused with a brigade of sixteen hundred soldiers at Soliseño Ranch. Soliseño is a town twenty-three miles west of Matamoros, and Soliseño Ranch, according to a 1903 map, was about a half-mile east of the town. On the 1853 river survey (the earliest available), it was about a quarter-mile south of a bend in the Rio Grande. That bend would have been about two miles from Las Rusias.[14]

He ordered them to cross the river as a vanguard for the rest of the army. They were to get between the US fort and the US supply base at Point Isabel and force General Taylor's outnumbered army to fight in the open. The crossing began on April 24.[15]

The stage was set.

CHAPTER 4

The Thornton Affair

As mentioned at the end of Chapter 1, moments before the Affair Captain Thornton's command had trooped into the plantation single-file, in the absence of any orders to remain outside on the road. Supervision thereupon ceased while Thornton—who should have supplied supervision—sought someone to talk to, to ask if the Mexican army had been spotted on this side of the river.[1]

The layout of the plantation was a rough semicircle with its flat side against the river. The perimeter fence was too high for most horses to jump and it was lined with dense brush, making jumping impractical anyway. Beyond the perimeter was the cart track they had followed to get to the entrance. Beyond that track was more brush. Inside the fence, the plantation was subdivided by a number of cross-fences short enough for a horse to jump. There were open spaces, clumps of brush, and a boggy pond.

Later, the survivors of Captain Thornton's command would agree that, after they trooped in, they ended up scattered in no order around some buildings about two hundred yards from the plantation's entrance. Some men were watering their horses, some were sleeping, some were smoking their pipes, and some were poking around the buildings. Maybe a third remained in the saddle.

The buildings were described alternately as houses or huts, and were probably *jacales* (pronounced ha-KAL-es), shacks whose walls were made of intertwined chaparral branches, covered with mud. They would not have interfered with visibility or offered defensible positions.

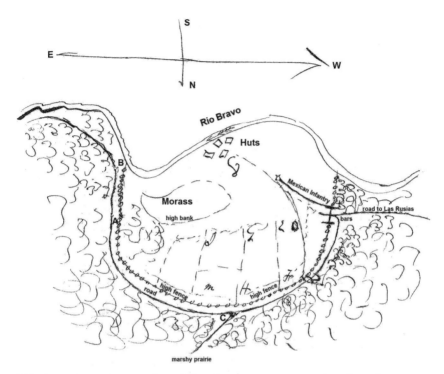

This is a cleaned-up version of the sketch map presented at Captain Thornton's court-martial, with certain labels replaced for legibility. Captain Thornton's patrol rode single-file from the east (the left) and after reaching point A turned back to the riverbank at point B. Having spotted a rider at point C, they proceeded there. (The meanings of the other reference letters were not recorded.) From C they followed the trail they found into the prairie. Seeing nothing, they returned to the road and continued west to the gate, labeled "bars," and then into the plantation to the huts. A few minutes later a large Mexican force began firing from the fence and pouring through the gate. Captain Thornton tried to lead a counter-attack that may be represented on the map by the line from the hand-drawn L to the hand-drawn D. Their horses stampeded, carrying them along the perimeter fence back to the east, going over at least one of the cross-fences (represented by dashed lines) and then toward the river. Captain Thornton's horse fell on him at an unrecorded spot. At the riverbank, in the absence of Captain Thornton, Captain Hardee organized a surrender. Credit: Author, National Archives

Some of the survivors said the jacales were on a hill, presumably meaning a bank of higher ground with better drainage. It likewise would not have been elevated enough to interfere with visibility or offer a defensible position. According to the map someone drew for Captain Thornton's court-martial, the jacales were near the river, in about the middle of the plantation's waterfront.

Then came the alert. Every man remembered hearing something different, from low-key announcements to instant panic.

Pvt. Frederick Lavoisien remembered turning his horse, seeing Mexicans at the gate, and trying to get the attention of various unit members. "There the Mexicans come," Lieutenant Kane remembered a sergeant announcing. Sergeant Clark just remembered hearing Captain Thornton yell, "Charge!"

On the other hand, Sergeant Freeman remembered hearing Thornton yell, "There are the Mexicans—thousands of them! Mount men, draw your sabers, and charge!" Pvt. William McConnell recalled Thornton yelling something less polite: "Jesus Christ there's thousands of them—draw your sabers, men, and charge!"

"Form, men, form, as well as you can," Captain Hardee began yelling.

They could now see that hundreds of Mexican troops, mounted and on foot, were lined up in the brush, outside the perimeter fence, on the far side of the cart track. Others were pouring through the gate at a run. Within moments a company of about one hundred Mexican infantry were through the gate and had formed up on the road leading to the jacales. They were facing away from the river, along the front of the fence, as if to fire into the flank of any troops that might attack the fence there from inside the plantation. Their right flank was exposed to the US force, but they could afford to do that since they were out of effective musket range. A formation of lancers was lined up in the road outside the gate.

As if on cue, Captain Thornton, gesturing with his saber, galloped toward the section of perimeter fence that the Mexican infantry was facing. (Another survivor mentioned that they were riding toward "the gap," so maybe there was a gap in the fence there, or a gap in the Mexican force.) He was riding as much as thirty yards ahead of the rest of his men. Only scattered shots were being fired until he was twenty or thirty yards from the fence, when he turned to see his men. Then a volley erupted and the horses of the men following him veered to the right and ran along the perimeter fence, away from the gate, completely out of control. Thornton's horse followed them to the right, also out of control.

Sergeant Freeman remembered that maybe fifteen men were mounted and able to immediately follow Captain Thornton. Then most of the rest of the men who were able to do so mounted and rode in that direction. After they headed off several of the remaining men began yelling, "Every man for himself!" Those simply scattered.

Back with Thornton the group continued following the perimeter fence to the right, under constant fire. If they weren't panicked their horses were. Thornton called for them to stop and tear down the fence, but none of them (including him) were able to stop their horses until they ran into an internal cross fence perpendicular to the perimeter fence. This they were able to jump.

On the other side, Lieutenant Kane recalled that his horse was hit by Captain Thornton's out-of-control horse and fell. Dismounted, he was trying to mount a loose horse when another out-of-control horse knocked him aside. About six men were with Thornton, he recalled. They and their horses then bolted off. Kane had snagged another horse and was trying to mount it when Hardee then came along with twenty or thirty men, and managed to pull up and asked if he were hurt—but then his horse knocked Kane over again. Hardee then rode off and Kane, still on foot, climbed over another fence and hid in the bushes, as he heard Mexican horsemen coming.

Thornton tried to ride along the perimeter to find another place to break through. Some second-hand accounts include dramatic scenes of him vaulting the fence and scattering the defenders as his horse was hit and fell. He himself only said that after a few moments his horse fell on him in a field and stunned him. (It was the same horse he'd ridden in Florida. It was a roan, meaning it had silver highlights.[2]) He was unable to rise. He could hear firing in the distance. Suddenly, it ceased.

That was because Captain Hardee had ridden with a group of men to the river and down along it, over a drop-off, through a cane brake, and into a field where he fell in with some other survivors gathered against the riverbank. He now had twenty-five men with him, or a little less than half the headcount that the squadron had had a few minutes earlier. As for the others, he assumed the worst.

The group was then out of range of the Mexicans and could reform. Captain Hardee asked if crossing the river was possible, and one man said he'd tried it but his horse mired on the bank.

Hardee then passed word around that the Mexicans might not accept a surrender, and they needed to be prepared to fight to the end and "sell their lives as dearly as possible."

"Who's for fighting?" he asked.

Basically, they weren't. "It's no use—we're surrounded," said one man. Others complained they had lost some or all of their weapons.

Hearing that, Hardee rode around and inspected their arms. Each man was supposed to have a carbine, a pistol, and a sword, but everyone had lost something, or everything, in the rush.

Someone proposed showing a white flag, presumably as more Mexicans came into view. Someone found a white handkerchief. Acquiescing, Captain Hardee sent a sergeant forward with the white handkerchief. A Mexican officer came forward. Hardee rode out to see him, and offered to surrender on condition of being treated as prisoners of war. The officer agreed. They dismounted and led their horses into captivity. Perhaps ten minutes had gone by since the shooting started.

Lieutenant Kane was found later in the bushes by a chain gang— some of the Mexican infantry were actually convicts in chain gangs. Thornton nowhere recorded what happened to him after his horse went down. Presumably he was in thick bushes where the Mexicans did not spot him. He was probably not under his horse, if only because the Mexicans would have been more likely to notice him. Another survivor recalled seeing it standing in a field, riderless, by the edge of the chaparral. After he was able to rise, the only way to get back to base would have been to proceed on foot down the road, where the Mexicans caught him the next day.

What may strike modern readers is that neither the subsequent court-martial nor the court of inquiry mentioned those who were lost. Of course, the trial was about the legal responsibility of the accused, and the court of inquiry was about the reputation of one survivor, and there was no need to dwell on anything else. But keep in mind that if there had been no losses there would have been no motivation to assign blame for those losses. So in a sense the dead must have been uppermost in everyone's mind.

Who were they? As usual with war fatalities, they were young men in the prime of life. Their backgrounds ranged from an ambitious scion to career privates, from a clerk to laborers, from across eastern North America to Ireland. By order of rank they were:

Second Lt. George Thomson Mason, twenty-seven, was in Company C. After finishing West Point in 1842 he had attended a US cavalry school and then had served in the 2nd Dragoons at Fort Jesup for a while. Then he had transferred to the 1st Dragoons (where his uncle was the commanding officer) and had been part of scouting expeditions out of Fort Leavenworth. Then he had returned to the 2nd Dragoons in 1844, in time for the war.[3]

First Sgt. George W. Smith of Company F, a Boston native, was thirty-four when he signed up on May 21, 1844, at Fort Jesup.[4] It was his second enlistment, implying he'd already been in the army for five years. He had blue eyes, brown hair and a fair complexion, and stood five feet eight inches tall.

Sgt. Javier Tredo of Company C had enlisted at age thirty-five, on October 5, 1844, at Fort Jesup. Despite his Latin name he was a Canadian native. For him, too, it was his second enlistment. He listed his occupation as soldier but at his age surely he'd had a previous one. He had blue eyes, sandy hair, and a dark complexion, and stood five feet seven inches tall. He died owing Mrs. Keane the laundress 75 cents, and the sutler $4.79. (A sutler was a merchant licensed to sell retail to the soldiers in camp. A laundress was attached to a company and received rations but no pay, which was to come from the men she served at fixed rates. If her services went beyond laundry she risked dismissal.)

Cpl. William Shaw of Company F was a farmer from Montreal, Canada, when he signed up at age twenty-three on August 9, 1844, at Fort Jesup. He had hazel eyes, dark hair, and a dark complexion, and stood five feet ten inches tall.

Pvt. John McGuire of Company C had enlisted May 27, 1842, at age twenty-one, in New York. He was from Boston, and had been a molder by trade. He had blue eyes, brown hair, and a ruddy complexion, and stood five feet nine inches tall. He died owing the sutler $4.26 (more than half a month's pay for a private) and 75 cents to Mrs. Keane.

Pvt. Thomas Fitzgerald of Company F had enlisted November 11, 1844, at age twenty-one in New Orleans. He was a laborer from Ireland. He had blue eyes, light hair, a fair complexion, and stood five feet nine inches tall.

Pvt. Isaac Hague of Company F was also an Irish laborer, from County Cavan. He enlisted at age twenty-seven on April 7, 1842, at Fort Braden, Florida, and was signed up by Captain Thornton himself. He had gray eyes, dark hair, and a fair complexion, and stood five feet nine inches tall.

Pvt. Jeremiah Healy of Company F was thirty when he enlisted on April 1, 1845, at Fort Jesup. It was his third enlistment, implying he'd already been in the army for ten years. Yet, he was still a private. He was a native of Columbia, Maine. He had gray eyes, brown hair, and a ruddy complexion, and stood five feet five inches tall.

Pvt. John Nagle of Company F, of County Cork, Ireland, was also starting his third enlistment when he signed up at Fort Jesup, at age thirty-five, on April 23, 1845. He had gray eyes, dark hair, and a dark complexion, and stood five feet eight inches tall.

There is no recorded gravesite for any of them.

Additionally, two enlisted men were recorded as wounded in the Affair, both from Company F. Pvt. Lewis Murray was a native of Litchfield, Connecticut, who was twenty-two when he was enlisted at Fort Fanning (modern Fanning Springs), Florida, by Captain Thornton himself, on February 24, 1842. He had gray eyes, brown hair, and a fair complexion, and stood five feet six inches tall. Despite his wound he served out his entire five-year enlistment.

Pvt. Patrick Connelly, a clerk from Ireland, was twenty-five when he signed up in New Orleans on June 4, 1845. He had gray eyes, dark hair, and a fair complexion, and stood five feet seven inches tall. At some point he was sent back to New Orleans, where he was given a certificate of disability and discharged on August 3, 1847.

The third person often listed as wounded was Captain Thornton himself, as his horse fell on him. There is no specific description of what his injury was, but he could easily have broken a leg.

However, that day he would have been considered missing, since no one knew where he was. Another soldier named James also temporarily avoided capture and was missing. So there were nine dead, two wounded and two missing—thirteen lost in combat out of fifty-five. Had the remainder been able to retreat and avoid capture, the loss would have been 24 percent.

CHAPTER 5

The Reports

THE DAY AFTER THE DEBACLE CAPTAIN HARDEE WAS BROUGHT TO Matamoros under guard, with the survivors of the patrol. He and Lieutenant Kane were lodged in a hotel. (There is no description of the treatment of the enlisted prisoners.) Hardee immediately wrote a report about what happened and was allowed to send it back to the US camp across the river that very evening. (Presumably, the Mexican authorities kept a copy for themselves.)

The next day Captain Thornton likewise was brought to the same hotel, and likewise wrote a report that was sent back to the US camp.

Back in Washington, emissary John Slidell returned to report the failure of his Mexican mission to President Polk on Friday, May 8—and spun it as a national insult that demanded an immediate declaration of war. Polk did not disagree, and held a Cabinet meeting the next day, Saturday, where he presented war as the next logical step. The Cabinet members were lukewarm. War was a big step, and negotiations with Britain about the status of Oregon were still ongoing, and there had been war talk on that front, too. (The Oregon issues were resolved two months later through bilateral negotiations.) Polk said he'd prepare a "war message" to present to Congress on Tuesday.

Then at 6:00 p.m. he got General Taylor's message with news of the Thornton Affair. Dated April 26, it stated that General Arista had returned and had sent Taylor an announcement that hostilities had commenced. And that a party of dragoons sent to patrol the river "appear to have been surrounded and compelled to surrender," incorrectly reporting sixteen killed and wounded out of a total of sixty-three.

"Not one of the party has returned, except for a wounded man sent in this morning by the Mexican commander, so I cannot report with confidence the particulars of the engagement or the fate of the officers . . ." he wrote. (Actually, two wounded men were sent.) He added that, hostilities having commenced, he had asked the governors of Texas and Louisiana to both send four regiments of volunteers, "to prosecute the war with energy and carry it, as it should be, into the enemy's country. I trust the department will approve my course in this matter. . . ." He than suggested that the volunteers should be enlisted for twelve months, rather than the usual six.[1]

Despite the hour, Polk called the Cabinet back into session. This time there was no push-back about declaring war. He and his staff rushed to prepare the war message for presentation a day earlier than planned.

Monday morning, a clerk spent ninety minutes reading the resulting lawyerly exposition to the House of Representatives. A sheaf of messages between Slidell and various Mexican officials was attached. These, apparently, were also read by the clerk. After brief debate the House approved President Polk's declaration of war and associated legislation 173 to 14. The Senate held out for another day, and then approved the measures by 40 to 2.[2]

The reports written by Captain Thornton and Hardee were not part of the message that triggered the declaration of war. Those were attached to General Taylor's subsequent message of May 3, reporting that he had retreated with his main force back to Point Isabel. However, the two reports have traditionally been the sole source of information about what happened, and historians have copied and paraphrased them, analyzed them, and extrapolated from them ever since.

That's unfortunate, since they were not only hastily written in the absence of any way of checking facts, but were written with the knowledge that the enemy would be reading them. Additionally, they both include self-serving distortions. Below we'll examine them to separate fact, fiction, and confusion. The non-annotated original reports, in the original formatting, are included in Appendix D.

Captain Hardee's report was dated April 26, 1846, from Matamoros, Mexico. Keep in mind that while Hardee had spent a brief tour in Florida after graduating from West Point in July 1838, he is not listed as having been in combat there. In 1846 he was known principally for having spent a year at a French riding school. The Thornton Affair was probably his first taste of combat, so it's no surprise that the report he wrote the next day shows signs of post-trauma stress.

It becomes my painful duty to inform you of the circumstances which led to our being brought to this place as prisoners of war. Capt. Thornton's command consisting of fifty-two dragoons left camp, as you know, at night on the 24th instant; it marched 15 miles and halted until daylight when the march was again resumed.

There were fifty-one troopers, four officers, and a guide, for a head-count of fifty-six. The error is not important, but is a warning that other facts in the report may be off.

Capt. Thornton's orders, as I understood them, were to ascertain if the enemy had crossed the river above our camp and to reconnoiter his position in force. All his inquiries on the way tended to the conviction that the enemy had crossed in strength. About 28 miles from our camp our guide became so satisfied of the fact that he refused to go any further and no entreaties on the part of Capt. Thornton could shake his resolution.

By "above of our camp" he meant "upstream of our camp."

Here, he introduces the idea that the disaster was caused by the overconfidence of Captain Thornton, who ignored reports of danger and as a direct result was now dead. Actually, the reports Thornton got were noise and he pressed on for that reason. Being at the end of the patrol's single-file column, perhaps two hundred yards back, Hardee could not have heard what was said, so his statements about what Thornton heard are pure conjecture. Meanwhile, twenty-eight miles was probably an overestimate.

About three miles from the latter place we came to a large plantation bordering on the river and enclosed with a high chaparral fence with some houses at the upper extremity.

By "upper extremity" he meant the opposite, upstream side of the plantation from where they encountered the plantation's perimeter, on the downstream side.

To these houses Capt. Thornton endeavored, by entering the lower extremity, to approach, but failing to do so was compelled to pass around the fence, and entered the field by a pair of bars, the houses being situated about 200 yards from the entrance.

By "bars" he means a fence gate consisting of bars that were slid back and forth to block and unblock the opening.

Into this plantation the whole command entered in single file, without any guard being placed in front, without any sentinel at the bars, or any other precautions being taken to prevent surprise.

This sentence was later taken out of context to be a complaint that Captain Thornton had not, on the march, used an advanced guard or flankers, despite orders to do so. Read in context, it was an observation of what happened after the patrol entered the plantation.

Capt. Thornton was prepossessed with the idea that the Mexicans had not crossed, and if they had that they would not fight.

Here he builds on his theme that the overconfident Captain Thornton was to blame. Of course, it is always dangerous to presume to know what another person is thinking. Thornton would later criticize him on this point.

I had been placed in rear and was therefore the last to enter, when I came up to the houses I found the men scattered in every direction, hunting for someone with whom to communicate. At last an old man was found, and while Capt. Thornton was talking to him the cry of alarm was given and the enemy was seen in numbers at the bars. Our gallant commander immediately gave the command to charge and himself led the advance, but it was too late, the enemy had secured the entrance and it was impossible to force it.

By "force it" he meant "drive its defenders away and gain control of it" rather than the modern usage of "pry it open."

The officers and men did everything that fearless intrepidity could accomplish, but the infantry had stationed themselves in the field on the right of the passageway and the cavalry lined the exterior fence and our retreat was hopelessly cut off. Seeing this Capt. Thornton turned to the right and skirted the interior of the fence, the command following him. During this time the enemy were shooting at us in every direction and when the retreat commenced our men were in a perfect state of disorder. I rode up to Captain Thornton and told him that our only hope of safety was in tearing down the fence, he gave the order, but could not stop his horse nor would the men stop. It was useless, for by this time the enemy had gained our rear in great numbers.

His rambling doubtless reflects the trauma he experienced. The prose should probably be read as his attempt to emotionally process the experience, rather than as a polished, sequential report.

Foreseeing that the direction which Captain Thornton was pursuing would lead to the certain destruction of himself and men without the possibility of resistance, I turned to the right and told them to follow me.

Here he's just repeating part of the previous paragraph, presumably because of his rattled nerves. But taken out of context, this statement makes it sound like Captain Hardee countermanded Captain Thornton's orders. It was evidentially one of the sources of the whispering campaign that he later sought to squelch by asking for a court of inquiry. But note that he earlier stated that Thornton had also turned to the right, presumably having also foreseen the same "certain destruction." The passage could be interpreted to just mean that he followed Thornton to the right and had the men do likewise.

> *I made for the river intending either to swim it or place myself in a position of defense. I found the bank too boggy to accomplish the former, and therefore rallied the men, forming them into order of battle in the open field and without the range of the infantry behind a fence.*

In other words, the riverbank was too muddy to ride their horses into the river, so they gathered at a spot on the riverbank out of effective range (i.e., anything over one hundred yards) of the Mexicans firing at them from the fence.

> *I counted 25 men and examined their arms, but almost everyone had lost a saber, a pistol, or carbine, nonetheless the men were firm and disposed if necessary, to fight to the last extremity. In five minutes from the time the first shot was fired the field was surrounded by a numerous body of men, however I determined to sell our lives as dearly as possible if I could not secure good treatment. Accordingly I went forward and arranged with an officer that I should deliver myself and men as prisoners of war and be treated with all the consideration to which such unfortunates are entitled by the rules of civilized warfare.*

Surrendering "at discretion" to the Mexican army, without making terms, had become synonymous with suicide. After the Alamo was stormed in 1836, the half-dozen survivors were killed out of hand. That had also been the fate of about 350 Texan rebels at Goliad a few weeks later, massacred after surrendering. Texan rebels defeated by a Spanish force outside San Antonio in the Battle of Medina of 1813 were also killed after surrendering, although the number is unknown. In 1842, thirty-six Texans died in the so-called Dawson Massacre when they proved unable to surrender during the Battle of Salado Creek outside

San Antonio. When nearly two hundred Texans escaped from a force that surrendered while conducting a counter-raid against Ciudad Mier three months later and were then recaptured, Santa Anna "compromised" by having only one in ten shot. They were selected through a lottery involving black and white beans. One of the black-bean-holders was merely wounded, faked death, and crawled away during the night, but was eventually hunted down and killed.

> *I was taken to a Gen'l. Torahon, who by this time had his full force collected in the field.*

"Torahon," of course, is his phonetic rendering of Torrejon, who led a brigade of about sixteen hundred men. Therefore, the patrol was out-numbered more than thirty to one.

> *I found that some prisoners had already been taken, which together with those I had, and those which were subsequently brought in amounted to 45 men exclusive of Lieut. Kane and myself. Four were wounded. I know nothing certain of the fate of Capt. Thornton and Lieut. Mason; the latter I did not see after the fight commenced. I am convinced they both died bravely, the former I know was unhorsed, and killed as I learned, in single combat by Roman Falcon.*

Someone miscounted. Under oath, in open court, Captain Thornton later indicated that the patrol (after Chipito's departure) had a headcount of fifty-five. Nine were now dead, and two others (Captain Thornton, and a private) were not captured that day, so there were only forty-four left. Of course, under the circumstances accuracy would have been an accident.

Meanwhile, Lt. Roman Falcon had been leading probes of the US forces since they reached the Arroyo Colorado. He was suspected (on no evidence) of killing Col. Trueman Cross, the army's chief quartermaster, while he was outside the camp horseback riding shortly after the army encamped opposite Matamoros.

Lieut. Mason's spurs were seen after the fight in possession of the enemy. The brave Sergeant Tredo fell in the first charge. Sergeant Smith was unhorsed and killed. The bodies of seven men were found including as I believe, the two officers above mentioned.

Nine men are known to have been killed outright, so they missed two bodies and misidentified one.

I was brought to Matamoros today about 4 o'clock, and I take pleasure in stating that since our surrender I and my brave companions in misfortune have been treated with uniform kindness and attention. It may soften the rigors of war for you to be informed fully of this fact. Lieut. Kane and myself are living with Gen'l. Ampudia: we lodge in his hotel, eat at his table, and his frank, agreeable manner and generous hospitality almost make us forget our captivity.

Presumably, the reason he dwells on this topic was because General Ampudia was famous for something other than generous hospitality. While previously he had had a command in the north, in 1843 he was sent to the Mexican state of Tabasco to put down a pro-federalist secessionist rebellion led by Gen. Francisco de Sentmanat. Suppressing it only took him a month, and General Sentmanat fled to the United States. Then, in May 1844, General Sentmanat returned with a filibustering expedition, apparently thinking he could retake Tabasco with seventy men. Ampudia quickly defeated this force. Then he hanged thirty-nine of them without trial, including Sentmanat. Still not satisfied, he had the head of Sentmanat severed, along with the heads of fourteen of his executed followers. He then boiled the flesh off their skulls and hung them in a local marketplace. One wonders what images were going through Hardee's mind while eating dinner with him.

Gen'l. Arista received us in the most gracious manner, said that his nation has been regarded as barbarous and that he wished to prove to us the contrary.

Arista's words may be a dig at Ampudia, whom Arista was known to despise. Or it may have involved awareness of the previously mentioned massacres.

Told Lieut. Kane and myself that we should receive half pay and our men should receive ample rations, and in lieu of it for today, 25 cents apiece. On declining the boon on the part of the Lieut. Kane and myself and a request that we might be permitted to send to camp for money, he said, No, that he could not permit it, that he intended to supply all our wants himself. These promises have already been fulfilled in full.

US Army officer rations were figured at 20 cents per day, so Arista's offer was quite generous.

The next day Thornton was brought in, demonstrably alive, and capable of understanding that Hardee had blamed the disaster on him. The look on the latter's face must have been memorable.

Thornton had seen death and disaster before, and his combat experience had doubtless taught him the purpose of military discipline—to maintain basic functioning in the face of chaos and mortal terror. So he functioned—he sat down and wrote a succinct, businesslike report. It, too, contains blame-shifting and errors, but they are subtler. It reached the US camp in time to be sent to Washington with Captain Hardee's report.

It was dated April 27, 1846, from Matamoros, Mexico.

I have the honor to report my arrival at this place today, and I state that agreeable with your orders I preceded to within three miles of La Rusia, when I was informed that the enemy had crossed in large numbers, upon receiving the information our guide refused to go any farther.

The place name is rendered "La Rusia" in the hand-copied version of his report included in the file of Captain Hardee's court of inquiry proceedings. As reprinted in the House Executive Documents[3] (since it was included in General Taylor's May 3 report to Washington), the place name is rendered as La Rosia. Neither is correct—the patrol was sent to Las Rusias. But since it was used in a printed government document, the name La Rosia lives on, unquestioned, and is even used by the semi-official history of the 2nd Dragoons.[4] The problem is that there is no location in the region called La Rosia. (There is a town in the region called La Rosita, but it's about one hundred miles west of Brownsville. And while there is also a La Rusia, it's another six hundred miles farther west in the Mexican state of Chihuahua.) Conjectures based on the report about the location of the Thornton Affair are inevitably inaccurate. (For other conjectures, see Chapter 12.)

> *I was therefore compelled to move on without him, in order to carry out your instructions to me. The advanced guard was increased and Lieut. Mason placed in command of it, with orders to keep about one quarter of a mile ahead, when we had gone about <two> miles, I discovered some Mexicans near a house in a large field, I halted the advance guard and went into the field myself to see them.*

The word "two" is illegible in the court of inquiry file, but is rendered that way in the Executive Documents.

> *I had not gone more than a hundred yards when they fled, I turned around and motioned to the advanced guard to come on, in the meantime the main body of the squadron had come up to the advance guard and mistaking my order, followed in after them, and while I was questioning a Mexican the enemy appeared.*

In other words, he says the main body would not have entered the gate if they had understood his orders. He does not say why he didn't correct the situation, but lets us believe that he was engrossed in the questioning of a prisoner, with the implication that his lapse was therefore excusable.

I immediately ordered a charge in order to cut my way through them, but finding their numbers too large to contend with any longer I ordered a retreat and although entirely surrounded we endeavored to cut our way through to camp. In the retreat my horse fell upon me and I was unable to rise.

While he implies that he launched an organized attack followed by an organized retreat, court testimony indicates a stampede that changed directions.

I'm now fully convinced that we were watched from the time we left camp and that preparations were so made as to prevent our ever returning.

In his later court testimony he was convinced that his guide, Chipito, led him into the ambush. While he was probably sincere, he was also ignoring the fact that the guide tried to get him to turn back, and later returned to camp alone.

It affords me great pleasure to say that the officers and men under my command both individually and collectively behaved in the most gallant manner. As a prisoner of war I am happy to inform you that attentions and kindness have been lavished upon me, and as an example of which I will state that upon my reporting to General Arista that a dragoon had treated me rudely, he ordered him immediately punished.

On the Mexican side, the defeat of Captain Thornton's command did not go unnoticed. General Torrejon sent back a report that was included in General Arista's April 26 report to the War Ministry.

As I began my march today, 1st Lt. Don Ramon Falcon, who since yesterday was on a scouting mission, informed me that an enemy advance party had been seen, and so I took action, and a few minutes later they were defeated by the forces under my command, who were eager to satisfy their justified animosity in the first encounter; though it has not been verified by officials in this report, the following were taken prisoner—a captain, a lieutenant, and 45 men, while the rest of the force was left dead on the battlefield and one drowned.[5]

Here again the number of prisoners (described as unverified) is said to be forty-seven when it must have been forty-four. Perhaps three men got counted twice. Presumably the Mexican count was the source of Captain Hardee's count, as he was probably not in any position to do any counting himself.

Note that there was no mention of any turncoat guide leading the US troops to slaughter—Lieutenant Falcon made contact, and the main force followed up. Meanwhile, there is no mention of a drowning victim in any other source. There was also no mention of Mexican casualties, presumably because there were none.

Back on the US side, Captains Hardee and Thornton were, sadly, not the only ones involved in blame-shifting. As mentioned, their reports were attached to General Taylor's May 3 report to Washington, written after he'd retreated back to Point Isabel.

A copy of my instructions to Captain Thornton, which will be furnished as soon as I again have access to my papers, will show that nothing was wanting on my part in the way of caution to that officer. I abstain from further comment, as a judicial investigation will no doubt be finally had in the case.

There was nothing about "the buck stops here," in other words. He then noted that the Texas Ranger camp was also hit by a surprise attack after they disregarded their commander's instructions. "Our men and officers have spirit enough, but lack prudence, which a little active service will soon teach them," he concluded.[6]

He apparently never did furnish a copy of his instructions to Captain Thornton—his next preserved messages to Washington concerned his victories at the battles of Palo Alto and Resaca de la Palma. There was then no longer any need to shift blame—and certainly no desire to revisit a time when he felt such a need.

But the pettiness and confusion preserved in their writings should be seen in context—they went on. Though what happened on April 25 was painful to them, as horsemen, they knew the importance of getting back in the saddle after a bad fall.

CHAPTER 6

The Two-Week Trans-Nueces War

CHIPITO RETURNED TO THE US BASE ON THE MORNING OF THE DAY after the Affair (i.e., Sunday, April 26, 1846) and reported that "all had been cut to pieces or taken prisoners."

Captain Thornton later cited Chipito's return as evidence that the guide had been in league with the enemy the whole time, since he otherwise could not have eluded them to get back. Of course, it's possible to make the opposite argument: Had he been in league with the enemy he would have had no reason to elude them and return. Either way, he drops from the record after that morning (aside from a rumor that he was later captured by the Mexicans and then pardoned by General Arista).

But Chipito's credibility stopped being an issue at about 11:00 a.m. when a cart came into camp carrying two wounded dragoons and a note from General Torrejon saying that "on the score of humanity he claimed the right of sending in two dragoons wounded in the affair of today, as he had no flying (i.e., mobile) hospital; that the officers and men would be treated with all the rights of prisoners of war, by orders of his chief."[1]

So General Taylor now knew that there was a powerful enemy force in his rear, free to strike either at his unfinished fort, or at his unfortified supply base at the Point Isabel port, or lay in wait for any road traffic between the two. His response was to ask the governors of Texas and Louisiana (the nearest states) for reinforcements. Or course, their arrival would take a couple of weeks at best. In the meantime he rushed to complete the fort, so he could leave a small force holding it while retreating out of that exposed position with his main force and return to the port, which was equally exposed but unfortified.

Another issue was that he had only a few days of food left for his army. That would not be a problem if he could send his supply wagons back to Point Isabel to be refilled from the ships there, but now there was a large enemy force in the way. He would have to use most of his force to protect the wagon train. On the other hand, the army would be easier to feed if he could get it back to Point Isabel. It could bring the irreplaceable wagon train with it. However, he didn't want to abandon the fort. A compromise was to leave a small force in the fort, which could live for a long time on the available supplies, and retreat with the remainder, taking the wagon train.

"Owing to the peculiar nature of the country and our deficiency in the proper description of light troops, I have been kept ignorant, to a great degree, of his (the enemy's) movements," he complained in his next report to Washington, written a week later, after he retreated to the port. "It was known, however, that he had crossed above in considerable force, as the unfortunate result of the reconnaissance conducted by Captain Thornton clearly showed. Owing to the unfinished state of the field work at our position, I could not prudently attempt any enterprise against this force for several days."[2]

So the next four days were spent finishing the earthwork, aiming to finish May 1.

Meanwhile, things got worse on the night of April 28 when a newly arrived Texas Ranger company camped near Palo Alto was surprised by General Torrejón's force. Five were killed and several others captured—and it was clear that a strong Mexican cavalry force was in place on the road between the fort and Point Isabel.

Word of its presence set off near panic at Point Isabel, where the local commander rushed to fortify the place with a scratch force of artillery-men, sailors, stevedores, and Texas volunteers, amounting to about four hundred. But General Arista did not press north up the road and try to use his three-to-one advantage to eliminate the US base. Instead, Arista had him loop around the US fort and return to the north side of the river opposite Rancho de Longoreño, about thirteen miles downstream from

Matamoros, to cover the crossing of the main Mexican force. Arista had heard rumors that Taylor was going to post sharpshooters on the riverbank to target Arista in his glittering uniform. So he wanted the north bank of the river cleared before he got there.[3]

The crossing commenced April 30, leaving a force of about fourteen hundred to hold Matamoros. General Arista's force could only find two suitable boats, so the process of crossing the river dragged on and on.

The next day, May 1, General Taylor learned of the crossing. The fort being provisionally complete, he got the bulk of his army on the road within two hours, leaving one infantry regiment, the sick, and three batteries of artillery (totaling about five hundred men) to hold the place. Instead of striking at the Mexican army while it was in a disorganized state astride the river, he rushed north to protect his port and refill his wagons. In other words, he adopted the previously mentioned compromise plan.

The US force sortied about 3:30 p.m., covered about ten miles, and camped about 11:00 p.m. at the Palo Alto watering hole. The name (Tall Timber) came from the fact that its clump of trees were the first trees a traveler encountered when coming from the coast. They pressed on the next day to Point Isabel, reaching it about noon, not having encountered the enemy.

Also on May 2 General Arista's force finally finished crossing the river, and he led it north to Point Isabel. He left a force to watch the US fort, commanded by his hated rival, General Ampudia.

On May 3 Arista reached the Palo Alto area and found that he had missed General Taylor. He was certain that Taylor would not abandon the US fort, and would soon return to resupply it. If he waited in the Palo Alto area for the US force to return, he could catch it in the open and use his numerical advantage. Then he could later mop up both the fort and the port.

So he decided to wait, and camped his army at another watering hole three miles to the southeast of Palo Alto, where he could cover the main road between Matamoros and Point Isabel road, plus another "fair weather road" to the east that (thanks to the clear weather) Taylor might use to return.

Also on May 3 the bombardment of the fort began, by artillery positioned in earthworks on the south side of the river. It continued during daylight for the next six days. Taylor's force at Point Isabel could clearly hear the guns, adding urgency to their task.

By the afternoon of May 7, General Taylor's soldiers had fortified the port and filled 270 supply wagons, and the force headed back to the fort. They went seven miles before camping that night.

About noon the next day (May 8, 1846) they reached Palo Alto. Their mounted scouts found General Arista's force deploying across the road ahead of them, having marched from their campground to the southeast. As they watched, General Arista's force was joined by General Ampudia's force coming north on the Matamoros road, having left the siege of the US fort.

The flat prairie offered no cover, while thick knee-high (and flammable when green) cord grass, scattered ponds, and muddy ground retarded off-road movement. Scattered, random clumps of chaparral brush offered minimal concealment, but denser thickets did limit visibility to the west and south.

Arista's force was on a line about a mile long, with most of the cavalry on the west. He had about thirty-seven hundred soldiers. Two eight-pounders and six four-pounders were scattered along the line.

The US force had about twenty-two hundred soldiers. They quickly deployed on a line about a thousand yards long, with the wagon train gathered in the rear. (The dragoons were on the left flank, and with the wagon guards.) Forced to divide his army between the fort and the field force, General Taylor had had to give up his balanced three-brigade organization and now faced the enemy with two improvised brigades. Being outnumbered by about 60 percent, he had to put nearly all his men in the line, leaving no significant reserve.

Basically, General Arista's plan had worked. He had caught the seriously outnumbered and dangerously isolated US force in the open. But beyond mere numbers another factor immediately came into play: technology. The US force had significantly superior artillery.

Taylor had two eighteen-pounders in the middle of the line, with enough range to reach most of the Mexican force. Additionally, there were two batteries of four six-pounders on each flank. The six-pounders were "flying artillery" trained by Maj. Samuel Ringgold. Following tightly choreographed drills, they would dash up to a point near the enemy but out of reach of effective musket fire, unlimber, quickly fire several shots, limber up, and dash away. They proved accurate enough to snipe at individuals.

The Mexican artillery began firing about 2:30 p.m. as the US force moved to within seven hundred yards. They fired solid cannonballs, that being the only ammunition they had for field artillery. The fire was largely ineffectual, as the balls had trouble reaching the US line without bouncing, presumably due to their weak gunpowder, as noted in Appendix B. Nevertheless, cannonballs could be deadly even when bouncing along the ground, and bouncing them was a tactic often used in battles of the gunpowder era when flat terrain was in play, turning the field into a nightmare bowling alley. But at Palo Alto it didn't work.

"They would strike the ground long before they reached our line, and ricocheted through the tall grass so slowly that the men would see them and open ranks and let them pass," recalled second lieutenant and future US president Ulysses S. Grant.[4] (He was in the infantry, near the middle of the line.)

The US artillery responded, reaching the enemy ballisticly (i.e., without bouncing) with all the precision afforded by 1846 technology, its limitations at least partially offset by the skill of the highly trained gunners. Their ammunition included solid cannonballs but also shells (which exploded in midair, raining scrap metal on the enemy) and canister (which turned the cannons into huge shotguns).

The utterly flat and almost featureless field quickly became a shooting gallery for the US artillery. General Taylor's infantry and mounted forces had little to do. For the Mexican soldiers, the results were ghastly, the fire opening "lanes" and "vistas" (as observers described it) through their formations.

The US artillery domination kept Arista from using his numerical advantage. He tried to send cavalry around the west flank, but they literally bogged down and were driven off. Operations halted between about 4:00 and 5:00 p.m. due to grass fires in no-man's-land. After operations resumed another attempt by a Mexican force to advance around the west was again driven off, but Major Ringgold was mortally wounded.

Arista then tried a final attack on the east flank. It was repelled by the usual storm of iron, and the retreating soldiers disrupted the Mexican line. With the sun setting, Arista decided to pull behind a chaparral thicket to the south, and the firing ended.

The US artillery had fired about three thousand rounds, while Arista's troops had fired about six hundred. US casualties amounted to six dead and forty wounded, or 2 percent. Mexican casualties were probably 10 to 15 percent. Despite the slaughter the Mexican soldiers had behaved as if they were on parade, yelling "Viva!" and closing ranks when shots took effect. At one point a regimental band began playing. The US artillery concentrated on it and immediately wiped it out.

During the night General Arista decided to put some distance between his army and the US force, so the next morning (May 9, 1846) he led it south six miles on the Matamoros road.

In the process he crossed several *resacas*, a feature common to the Rio Grande's alluvial delta. Sometimes referred to as ravines, resacas are silted former riverbeds of the Rio Grande, usually about four feet deep with flat, marshy bottoms, sometimes with ponds, and fifty or more yards wide. The foliage that grew along the riverbank mostly remained standing after the river relocated. The result could be seen as a natural, camouflaged trench, albeit one that was too wide for easy flank defense.

At the sixth mile the road crossed Resaca de Guerrero (Guerrero being the landowner) at Charca de la Palma (Palm Pond). Arista deployed his forces in and behind the resaca on either side of the road. There they could take cover from the US artillery. His line extended about a thousand yards on either side of the road, with seven cannons covering the crossing, lined up just in front of the resaca. He assumed that by the time the US force arrived and deployed it would be too late to fight that day. Meanwhile, the bombardment of the fort, three miles to the south, could continue.

The chaparral had become increasingly prevalent as they marched south, and by Resaca de Guerrero the terrain was a continuous dense thicket. There was a cleared corridor through the chaparral on either side of the road, made by wood-cutters, about fifty yards wide. The Mexican artillery covered the approach through this corridor.

Taylor spent several hours fortifying his wagon train, and then followed Arista's force, making contact on the approach to Resaca de Guerrero about 2:00 p.m. His officers mistook the name of the place as Resaca de la Palma and gave that name to the entire riverbed and to the resulting battle, and so it remains in US histories and on US maps. It remains Resaca de Guerrero in Spanish-language materials.

Despite General Arista's expectations, General Taylor immediately attacked, while deploying units as they arrived to the right and left. The Mexican artillery fire coming down the road corridor became a problem, so Taylor sent in the dragoons to take the guns.

The attack was led by Capt. Charles May—the same one who got his commission because President Jackson liked the way he rode a horse, and whose lost position at the head of the regiment's road column outside Crockett, Texas, Major Fauntleroy had pointlessly rushed to restore.

Captain May put himself at the head of two companies lined up four men wide and twenty deep, and launched a very un-dragoon-like Napoleonic cavalry charge that swept over and round the guns, capturing them and a Mexican general. However, neither the guns nor the general could be secured until the supporting infantry arrived.

Dragoon Private Milton later told a rapt newspaper interviewer that he was unable to get his horse to vault the guns (he was in the dragoons, after all, not the cavalry) so he rode around the guns and into the resaca. There, he encountered dust, smoke, and unbounded madness. A Mexican lancer made a run at him, Private Milton parried the lance with his sword, the lance only grazed him, and the lancer fled. Then a shot killed his horse and wounded him in the leg. The horse fell on his good leg. Another mortally wounded horse thrashed about and seemed to be about to fall on the trapped private, and finally went down a yard away. Private Milton then took another bullet in his ankle, and fainted. He was roused to find a wounded Mexican soldier crawling toward him, calling to him, and pressing into his hands a certificate indicating the bearer was, as of April 13, the member of a regular cavalry unit. Did he think surrendering required paperwork? Perhaps he was hoping to differentiate himself from the Mexican irregulars, one of whom appeared out of the dust and began killing and robbing wounded men from both sides using a US Army sergeant's short sword he'd picked up. With great difficulty Private Milton pulled out a loaded pistol to bear on the perpetrator—but then something else scared the human vulture away. Two hours later he and the wounded Mexican cavalryman were rescued by US forces.[5]

US forces gained control of the resaca because, while all the excitement was in progress on the road corridor and in the resaca, the infantry that peeled off to the right (i.e., west) soon encountered the defended lip of the resaca, as it ran parallel to the road there. (Those who went into the chaparral to the east found, mostly, more chaparral.) Countless small-unit actions broke out. Later arrivals found a cow path across the resaca that put them beyond the Mexican west flank. Acting on their own initiative, they pressed their advantage and rolled up that flank of General Arista's force. Soon his whole position likewise collapsed and his army was in disorganized flight back to the river, pursued by some of the US dragoons who managed to get reorganized.

General Taylor was able to link up with the fort that evening. Finding that its commander, Maj. Jacob Brown, had died earlier that day after being hit by a shell on May 6, he named the earthwork Fort Brown.

Ignoring the anonymous infantrymen who waded into the tall chaparral knowing an unseen enemy was in there waiting for them, the US public thereafter lionized Captain May and his mounted charge. His face (with the long hair and beard he'd been wearing that day) became a national icon. (He was usually depicted vaulting a Mexican gun with his personal horse—the thing Private Milton's government-issued horse had refused to do.) He's mentioned in the fourth stanza of "Maryland My Maryland" since his parents were from Baltimore. He got a brevet promotion of two grades, to lieutenant colonel.[6] (There was no other system of merit awards at the time.)

As for the price of glory, eighty men took part in that charge, and nineteen were lost—nine killed and ten wounded. That's 24 percent, which would have been considered catastrophic had the enemy not been defeated. Ironically, it's the same loss rate as Captain Thornton's patrol, disregarding the subsequent capture of the remainder. (The much larger

"Charge of the Light Brigade" during the Crimean War eight years later, involving the inadvertent commitment of an unsupported light cavalry unit to a frontal assault on an artillery position, resulted in 40 percent casualties.)

Army-wide, US casualties were forty-five killed and ninety-eight wounded. Two men, including Major Brown, had died in the fort during the bombardment. Mexican casualties were listed as 154 killed, 205 wounded, and 156 missing.[7]

US reinforcements and heavy rain arrived in the next days. There was a prisoner exchange on May 11, and Captains Thornton and Hardee, plus their men, were returned to the US Army. On May 17 General Arista abandoned Matamoros to retreat about two hundred miles to Linares, leaving about four hundred wounded. He started the hastily organized march with about four thousand soldiers and arrived eleven days later with only 2,638.[8]

The Trans-Nueces War (the one that Generals Arista and Taylor thought they were fighting) was now over. The US Army had demonstrated its control over the disputed territory. Mexican attempts to demonstrate otherwise had failed. Logic demanded that diplomats now earn their pay, as the soldiers had just done, and tie up the results with a grandly worded treaty recognizing the new border. The dead would be buried and life would go on.

It didn't happen that way. Leaders on both sides scrambled to pursue agendas unconnected with whether the Rio Nueces or the Rio Grande was the legitimate border. The Trans-Nueces War was over but the Mexican-American War had just begun. The results would transform both nations.

As for Captain Thornton, it would provide a forum to clear his name, and then an opportunity to test his luck further. The first ended well, the second less so.

CHAPTER 7

The After-Affair in Court

GENERAL TAYLOR'S ARMY STAYED IN MATAMOROS FOR THE NEXT THREE months, into August, trying to absorb an influx of reinforcements. When Congress declared war after getting word of the Thornton Affair (as mentioned), it had authorized that companies should be expanded to one hundred men, and increased the overall size of the US Army by a factor of six.

Meanwhile, there was time for ancillary activities, including courtroom trials.

Captain Hardee found that the report he'd written in his hotel room in Matamoros while a prisoner of war had not made him popular in the army. This was not because it was sent to Washington and triggered a declaration of war, but because it contained statements that contradicted the report of Captain Thornton, his superior. Also, by gathering the survivors around him and surrendering he appeared to have undercut Thornton's authority. (Apparently, any officer in camp could go to headquarters and read all the reports.)

Hardee must have moved fast, as he returned to the army in a prisoner exchange on May 11 and the court was organized, and convened by the end of the May. He was a ball of nerves throughout the proceedings, resorting to written statements at odd moments. Thornton testified on his behalf—more or less. In the end Hardee got what he wanted—the court whitewashed both his report and his actions.

Then it was Captain Thornton's turn—he found himself courtmartialed for negligence and for disobeying orders in the conduct of the patrol. A general court-martial started hearing his case on June 10, a few days after Hardee's hearing wrapped up. His defense was amazingly sedate, as befits a man acclimated to facing death. (Also, this was his fourth appearance in front of a military court.) Hardee testified on his behalf—tepidly, but he said the right things. In the end Thornton was acquitted—but not totally cleared of neglect.

Captain Hardee's day in court (actually the proceedings dragged on over eight days) was, as mentioned previously, a court of inquiry rather than a criminal trial. Courts of inquiry were held to inquire into a problem, establish the facts, and sometimes suggest further action. However, a court of inquiry could summon witnesses and have them testify under oath, just like a court-martial. To avoid political manipulation, courts of inquiry could only be ordered by the commander-in-chief (i.e., the president of the United States), or by a commanding officer at the request of an accused person in his command. In this case Hardee felt he'd been accused of various things by the rumor mill and his commanding officer, General Taylor, agreed to convene a court. (The full transcript appears in Appendix D.)

Such courts also had fewer members (three) than did a general court-martial (thirteen) and in this case there were two from the infantry and one from the artillery. They began meeting on May 25, empowered to "examine into the nature of certain imputations affecting his [Capt. Hardee's] character as connected with his conduct in the engagement between Capt. Thornton's command and the Mexicans on the 25th ultimo, and also to examine and inquire upon certain statements contained in his official report of said engagement."

Captain Hardee began with a written statement, saying that he sought to show that his report did not contradict that of Captain Thornton, and that he wanted to counter "imputations of an infamous nature (that) have by some individuals at least been made with more or less publicity against me." Although he doesn't state it until later, these "imputations" were that he had countermanded Thornton's orders during the retreat.

Lieutenant Kane testified first, laying out what happened during the patrol, how they went upriver during the night, rested, and resumed the next morning, never getting a straight answer to their questions. Then the guide took fright and left. They pressed on, found the plantation, poked around outside it and then went inside it, and started milling around. Then the ambush happened, and there was no possibility of a organized resistance.

Kane told of being present when Thornton met Hardee in Matamoros and Thornton was told what was in Hardee's report. (Apparently he did not actually show him a copy, assuming Hardee had one.)

"He [Capt. Thornton] had some slight objection to the report of a want of caution, saying that we had done all we could do, and that he did not care a damn what was said provided his reputation for gallantry for preserved," Kane testified.

That consumed the first day. (Proceedings usually began at 10:00 a.m. and ran until about 2:00 p.m., presumably adjourning for a late lunch.)

On the second day Captain Thornton testified on behalf of Captain Hardee, giving the outline of events. When, after the Mexicans attacked, he tried to get his men to halt and tear down the fence, he heard Hardee repeat the order, implying Hardee wasn't trying to subvert him.

He then said he had not read Hardee's report, and was shown a copy and asked if he had any problems with it.

He responded, "Capt. Hardee is mistaken in that portion of his report, 'Capt. Thornton was prepossessed with the idea that the Mexicans had not crossed, and if they had they would not fight.'" (Of course, he could not have known what Captain Thornton was thinking. Anyway, Thornton's actions showed that he anticipated having to fight.)

Less reasonably, he then added, "That portion of the report which states, 'When I came up to the houses, I found the men scattered in every direction,' is a decided inaccuracy.'" Maybe they weren't scattered in every direction when Thornton got there, but that's because he was at the head of the column. When Hardee, at the end of the column, got there, they were indeed scattered in every direction. All the other witnesses, at this hearing and later at Thornton's court-martial, agreed on that point.

More reasonably he stated, after reading further, "'Seeing this Capt. Thornton turned to the right and skirted the interior of the fence, the command following him,' is inaccurate. The squadron, or a portion of it, had turned to the right, and were going up the fence, when I turned my horse and followed after it." Of course, this is splitting hairs—the situation was out of control.

Hardee then asked Thornton if he hadn't said, on that road, that he would believe that the Mexicans had crossed when he saw them? And that when fighting the Mexicans he wanted his men armed only with whips (i.e., as if to drive cattle)? While it sounds like he was trying to embarrass Thornton, keep in mind that Thornton was not the one on trial. Hardee was probably trying to establish grounds for having stated in his report that Thornton did not, that day, believe the Mexicans had crossed or would fight.

To the first question, Thornton answered that he might have said such a thing—before the guide took fright and fled. To the second he said he had frequently said it in camp, but not on this occasion.

At any rate, Thornton didn't sound offended—his final statement was that yes, in Matamoros, he had told Hardee that he had done well in surrendering the squadron. "That is, that he had pursued a correct course as I believed the retreat was cut off," he testified.

That ended the second day. The third day involved testimony from three enlistment men about the events of April 25th. Under questioning, they said there was no concerted action in response to the attack and troopers in the ranks were yelling, "Every man for himself!"

On the fourth day two more enlisted men testified about the chaos triggered by the Mexican ambush, and then Hardee read a written statement inviting the court to call additional witnesses if it wished. There is no immediate reaction, and he then called several officers to testify concerning the rumors that were spreading in camp about him.

An infantry officer testified that people were saying, "It was evident that he, Capt. Hardee, had deserted his commanding officer and carried off 25 men with him." Also, "There was direct contradictions between the official report presented by Capt. Hardee and that presented by Capt. Thornton."

Capt. Charles May—now famous for leading that bloody charge at Resaca de la Palma—also testified that he'd heard people bad-mouthing Hardee. He, too, had heard that there were contradictions between the two reports, and that Hardee had deserted his commanding officer and carried off twenty-five men.

"That I have heard it very harshly spoken of, and that I myself believed and spoke of it, that Capt. Hardee had assumed a responsibility that his commission did not entitle him to," May said. "The opinions that I heard expressed, and that I expressed myself, was formed from his own report." (The fact that he was testifying for Hardee implied he no longer held those opinions.)

Colonel Twiggs, the commanding officer, was also called. He said he himself had said nothing bad about Hardee but had heard others complain. "It was in this, that when Capt. Thornton ordered a charge, Capt. Hardee gave different orders, and for this he was censorable," he said. As for the reports, some officers complained that one report said there was an advanced guard, and the other said there wasn't, he noted.

They skipped the fifth day—Captain Hardee wasn't ready. On the sixth he read a thirty-six-hundred-word statement tediously reviewing everything the witnesses had said, to demonstrate that his report had not conflicted with Captain Thornton's, and that he had not subverted Thornton's orders. Concerning the latter, Hardee observed that he'd been incautious in the way he stated that he had the men follow him away from certain destruction, and the statement had been misconstrued. But all was chaos and the commanding officer was not in sight when he did that, the witnesses agreed. In the end all he did was rally some fugitives, he explained.

The court then agreed to summon six men at random who had been part of the patrol that day.

The seventh day of testimony took place three days later, as some of the men had to be summoned from Point Isabel. The six selected men were each asked (among other things) what formation the squadron was in when it entered the plantation, what commands they heard Captain Hardee give, and what his behavior was like during the affair. He stepped outside while the last question was being posed.

They typically responded that there was no formation, they heard no commands after the shooting started, and they thought Captain Hardee was a brave man who did the best that he could in the circumstances.

The court then deliberated and issued the opinion that Hardee sought: that his conduct during the affair was "that of an intelligent and gallant soldier, that he did all in his power, by word and deed, to sustain his commanding officer in the discharge of his duty, and that any imputation against his character, growing out of his conduct as connected with that affair, is utterly without foundation." It also found that his report was correct in all particulars.

The court-martial of Captain Thornton began on June 10, 1846. (The full transcript is in Appendix E.) It was a general court-martial, and it also heard the case of Col. William Whistler, who is not otherwise mentioned in the file, but who was apparently tried after Thornton. Colonel Whistler was the uncle of the artist James Abbott McNeill Whistler, painter of "Whistler's Mother." Colonel Whistler was convicted of drinking on duty, but was later returned to duty by President Polk due to the army's shortage of officers.[1]

Thornton got permission for Bvt. Capt. Philip Barbour, 3rd Infantry, and Lt. Braxton Bragg, 3rd Artillery, to attend as his counsel. The former was killed in action three months later. The latter later became a Confederate general and commander of the Army of Tennessee, and his erratic bumbling and feuding pretty much assured Union victory in the western theater. However, the transcript shows that only five questions were posed by counsel. They probably, however, helped Thornton compose his defense summation.

He was charged with neglect of duty and disobedience of orders. He neglected duty in that he "did omit the necessary and customary precautions, to secure his command against surprise, and did suffer it to be ambuscaded, and entirely cut off by a large force of the Mexican Army." He disobeyed orders in that he had been instructed to (among other things) "move with the utmost caution, keeping out advanced and flank guards, and taking the greatest care not to be drawn into an ambuscade."

No violation of the Articles of War was cited, but the offenses presumably fell under the catch-all Article 99, for non-capital offenses against good order and military discipline not otherwise specified. Punishment was purely at the discretion of the court.

General Taylor testified that Captain Thornton reported to him for orders, and he told the captain that the point was to see if reports about the Mexican force and its position were true. He does not mention what those reports were, or why the patrol was being sent to Las Rusias, but presumably he'd heard of the Mexican forces that were massing at Soliseño, across the river from the Las Rusias area.

"My object in sending the command was information," the general testified. "That if he met with a small party he might capture them, but if in force to avoid them. That he would keep out a small front and flank guard, and thoroughly examine every place with a few men, whenever there was a possibility of an ambush being made before he committed his command. That it would be better to rush and sacrifice a few than the whole, but should he get surrounded he would cut his way through and return to camp." Some other officers testified of overhearing the same conversation, and then Hardee was called as a witness for the prosecution.

He did not stab Thornton in the back. He described the general course of events, but said he did not know if there was an advance guard as ordered, as he was at the rear of the column. As for flank guards, he said the brush was so thick they were not possible. He stated that no guard was placed on the gate after they entered the plantation, and inside the plantation the men were not in formation—but he only said that when specifically asked. When asked if the command was "entirely cut off," he skirted the question, only noting that all but two were captured immediately.

Lieutenant Kane and Sergeant Lenz were also called to give an account of the events, ending the first day's testimony.

On the second day the prosecution called Pvt. James Orr, who was found to be intoxicated and placed in confinement. (This may have been the other trooper who evaded immediate capture during the Affair.)

They then called Pvt. William McConnell, who apparently was not intoxicated and told of the unit's disorder inside the plantation. But when asked, he said he heard no order to dismount, or any permission to take a break.

The prosecution then rested, and Hardee was immediately called back as a defense witness. He said that, being at the end of the column, he didn't know much about Thornton's security measures, but implied that they didn't matter, as the patrol was doomed anyway.

"From the nature of the country through which we passed, and information I subsequently derived from Mexican officers, of which there could be no doubt, the squadron would in my opinion have been entirely cut to pieces if it had not gone into the field," he testified. He added that he was told while a prisoner that the patrol had been watched from the time it left camp. However, he also said that he did not think that Chipito had betrayed them.

Kane was then brought back to testify about Thornton's security precautions and use of an advanced guard—riding with Thornton, he'd seen them. But he also stated, in response to questions, that Thornton was not paying any attention to the squadron as it entered the plantation, as he was absorbed trying to gather information. Had the main body of the squadron followed directions and kept its distance from the advance guard it would not have entered the plantation, and would have waited on the road outside. And there they would have all been killed. They were surrounded and Chipito had betrayed them, he said.

That ended the second day. On the third day nothing related to the case took place. On the fourth day, July 15, 1846, Thornton presented his thirty-five-hundred-word defense summation, apparently read by one of his counsels.

The summation once more went over the course of events, and noted that maybe he should have turned back when Chipito did. But he had nothing to report—and it is likely he would have walked into an even more disastrous ambush on the way back. He added that he went into the plantation alone, "determined not to risk the safety of an individual of my command by taking any of them into the field until it became necessary." His attention was on the Mexicans fleeing the houses, and he beckoned backward, without looking, for the advanced guard to follow, he said. If the main body had not closed up they would not have followed. With them waiting outside, there would have been no need to post sentinels at the gate, he noted.

He also noted that carrying out the mission in fifteen hours, over-night, in strange country, was difficult, and that commanding the squadron and gathering information were incompatible jobs. Meanwhile, the enemy was constantly spying on them, but the US forces had no way to spy on the enemy. But the loss of the squadron revealed the enemy's deployments and the peril the army was in, he noted.

"If, gentlemen, I neglected any necessary or usual precautions to secure my command, it must have resulted from a want of knowledge," he concluded. "And I pray you, therefore, they acquit me of the [charge of] neglect, and, if necessary, render your verdict against me for incapacity. . . . If I had disobeyed an order, it is the first time in my life, and I hope I am not too sanguine in concluding that literal obedience in this instance was impossible, and its attempt inevitable destruction. Mr. President and Gentleman, my military reputation—my honor—my all—is committed to your keeping. Your country has found hers safe in your hands, and, with the confidence which that is calculated to inspire, I submit my case to your decision."

The court then retired, deliberated, and returned with a verdict. They decided he had taken the "necessary and customary precautions, in all respects performed his duty as a commander, to the period of time when the troops entered the field referred to in the testimony."

He had not thereafter taken the necessary precautions, the court noted, but this lapse had had nothing to do with the squadron being ambushed. So he was found not guilty of the first specification and therefore of the first charge, of neglect of duty.

For the same reason he was found not guilty of the second specification and therefore of the charge of disobeying orders.

So he was acquitted. Captain Thornton still had his career. But, basically, the court let him off because it appeared that the patrol had been doomed anyway. The testimony from Captain Hardee and Lieutenant Kane, despite embarrassing elements, had the overall effect of backing him up.

"Capt. Thornton was honorably acquitted by the court, and it was universally conceded that although there may have been errors of judgment, yet that the dragoons—officers and men—without exception, displayed the utmost gallantry," concluded the regiment's historian in 1875.[2]

CHAPTER 8

Thornton's Final Luck

GENERAL TAYLOR'S ARMY MOVED UPSTREAM IN AUGUST, TOOK MON-
terrey in late September, and eventually pushed on to Saltillo. There were
no more massed cavalry charges—the US Army could not afford to use
its horsemen as projectiles, much as the public loved the spectacle. For
instance, the US Army lost almost five hundred men taking Monterrey,
but only two were from the 2nd Dragoons, as the unit was used only for
security and patrolling.

Meanwhile, other expeditions went on to seize essentially all the
Mexican territory that President Polk had offered to buy.

Then—not for the last time—the US found that superior training,
equipment, and logistics could produce lopsided military victories but not
necessarily an exit strategy. The Mexican government showed no inclination to come to terms. Indeed, that parts of the country were occupied by
armies commanded by generals who did not answer to Mexico City was
not a new or alarming development in Mexican politics.

In response, the Polk Administration made two pivotal decisions.
The first was to let Santa Anna pass through the US naval blockade and
return to Mexico, where he arrived August 16, 1846. While the decision
seems disquietingly naive in light of what followed, Santa Anna had been
quite helpful up to that time, and the United States was actually following the strategy he laid out. The Polk Administration assumed he would
re-establish control of Mexico and make peace. He did re-establish control—and then proceeded to prosecute the war with renewed vigor. It's
possible that he discovered that Mexican public opinion was such that he

could not stay in power if he made peace. Or, he could have been playing Polk like a violin.

The second decision was that the United States would need to "conquer a peace" by seizing the enemy capital and dictating terms. This would involve landing an army on the coast and moving inland 250 miles through enemy territory, much of it rugged. It would be a feat reminiscent of Hernando Cortez in 1520, without the decisive technological and disease-related advantages he enjoyed. They may not have understood the scale of hubris their plan involved, but they did decide to improve the odds by stripping most of the veteran regular units from General Taylor's army. They moved them to the coast to take part in the invasion. Taylor was largely left with a collection of state militia units. Meanwhile, the Polk Administration rushed to organize an amphibious invasion of Mexico before the summer of 1847, as the army would have to move inland before the summer's yellow fever season started on the coast.

Santa Anna got wind of this plan. By supreme effort he concentrated an army of about twenty thousand soldiers against Taylor and his largely green force. He marched his army 240 miles across a desert in winter and attacked the US force in rugged terrain south of Saltillo. Despite having a three-to-one numerical advantage, Santa Anna lost the resulting Battle of Buena Vista/Angostura (February 23, 1847). By the time he'd retreated across the same desert with worse logistics than he'd had during the advance, Santa Anna had lost, in the course of the campaign, half his army. But he wasn't pursued (Taylor knew about that desert) and he'd captured two small artillery pieces, so he claimed victory.

Three companies of the 2nd Dragoons had been left with Taylor, under the now famous Bvt. Lt. Col. Charles May. Again, he avoided doing anything rash at Buena Vista/Angostura and only two dragoons were wounded.[1]

Meanwhile, the invasion force gathered on the Texas coast.

Opening its attempt to take Mexico City, a US force commanded by Gen. Winfield Scott conducted an amphibious landing, using specially made barges, on an open beach just south of Vera Cruz on March 9, 1847. The landing was not opposed, and Scott was soon able to lay siege to the port of Vera Cruz with a force of thirteen thousand men.[2]

The dragoons consisted of six companies, taken from both the 1st and 2nd Dragoon Regiments,[3] including those of Captains Thornton and Hardee. Initially they didn't fare well, having lost some of their horses before the landing when they were washed overboard in a storm. Nevertheless, they managed to hold off probes from inland. The city surrendered on March 29, yielding about five thousand prisoners, including six generals and eighteen colonels—more than enough brass to command the pre-war US Army.

Eager to get away from the coast before summer, Scott had his force start moving inland on April 2, using a highway that followed the same route that Cortez had used. Due to a shortage of draft animals, Scott was initially limited to marching with eighty-five hundred men.

By April 12 they were probing a fortified defile just beyond the edge of the yellow fever belt where the highway passed through some abrupt hills, about fifty-five miles from Vera Cruz, just east of the village of Cerro Gordo (Fat Hill). There, Santa Anna (just returned from putting down an uprising in Mexico City unconnected with the broader war) had massed a scratch force of about twelve thousand men.

While General Scott's main force confronted the Cerro Gordo position, his engineers established a route through the trackless hills on the right (i.e., to the north) that a flanking force could use to get behind Santa Anna. (Capt. Robert E. Lee was heavily involved.) About 7:00 a.m. on April 18 Scott, with a force of about eighty-five hundred, attacked the main defenses from both sides and by 10:00 a.m. the Mexican force had disintegrated. More than three thousand were taken prisoner. Pursuit with mounted forces continued until evening.

Captain Thornton and his dragoons were heavily involved in the pursuit, pressing about seven miles up the highway to a place they called Hacienda El Encero (actually, Hacienda El Lencero) and then a couple of miles beyond, toward Jalapa. (They missed Santa Anna, who fled almost alone to the south, although others captured his parade dress wooden leg.) The dragoons were then recalled and told to camp for the night at the hacienda.

No one seemed to take much note of the fact that the hacienda was on one of Santa Anna's personal estates. What they did take note of was Captain Thornton's behavior during the pursuit of the enemy that afternoon, as he could barely stay on his horse, rode out of ranks, and did erratic things.[4] That evening, while their servants made supper, Thornton had gotten into a childish argument with another officer. Captain Hardee, fearing they would come to blows (or just acting on his West Point/École Royale de Cavalerie instincts) put them under arrest. Thornton talked back to Hardee, saying they were not fighting, he had no right to do this, that he, Thornton, was arresting Hardee, etc.

Hardee was about to go off and find Major Beall, who was in charge of the mounted troops, and report the matter—but then his servant served supper. Ever the finicky eater, he stopped everything, sat down, and ate. Meanwhile, Thornton went off, and then returned, saying he'd talked to Beall, and things were all right and Hardee was under arrest.

Hardee duly finished eating and himself went off and found Major Beall, who said he'd confirmed the arrest of Thornton and the officer he'd been arguing with. Hardee then went to his quarters and later heard that Beall had released the other two from arrest.

So, on a day when the US Army managed to crush a numerically superior force that was dug in across its path in rugged terrain, scatter it, turn Santa Anna into a fugitive, and leave nothing between themselves and central Mexico, Captain Thornton distinguished himself by appearing drunk and breaking arrest.

At the time, the US force could not be bothered with such trivia. The next day they pressed on another seven miles to Jalapa, and there General Scott had to face a disaster—the enlistments of seven regiments of volunteers who signed up a year earlier, right after the Thornton Affair, were expiring. Only a fraction proved willing to re-enlist, the rest having had enough excitement. Scott suddenly lost three thousand men, leaving him deep in enemy territory with only seven thousand men.[5]

Guerrilla activity on the road back to Vera Cruz was such that Scott could not stay where he was and still maintain a connection with the coast. So, in a move of astonishing boldness, he decided not to bother with a connection. He pressed on into the interior, paying cash for supplies and making friends with local power brokers, especially the church. It worked. He still periodically received supplies (especially ammunition and money) and reinforcements from the coast. They would fight their way inland in brigade-sized formations. More than one basically re-enacted the Battle of Cerro Gordo, albeit on a smaller scale.

On May 15, brushing aside light resistance, the army reached Puebla, 107 road miles inland from Jalapa, the second largest city in Mexico and two-thirds of the way to Mexico City.[6] There they remained for the next ten weeks as Scott sought to rest and refit his force, wait for reinforcements, handle neglected administrative chores, and negotiate with and/ or bribe Santa Anna.

Treating with Santa Anna proved fruitless. He remained unmoved after getting a $10,000 cash bribe. It was well known that the US Congress had appropriated $3 million to "facilitate negotiations" and many parties were avidly anticipating some of that facilitation, but the US authorities primly conceived it as funding for the Mexican government after it surrendered.[7]

On the other hand, the rest, refitting, and absorption of reinforcements by Scott's force went well. As for the administrative chores, a general court-martial was convened May 30, 1847.

Captain Thornton was faced with four charges. The first accused him of "conduct prejudicial to good order and military discipline," and violating Article 52 of the Articles of War, concerning misbehavior before the enemy. The latter was a capital offense. The specifications said that Thornton, "while in the hot pursuit of the enemy on the 18th day of April 1847, from the Cerro Gordo, Mexico, and expecting every moment to overtake and engage them, was drunk." The second specification said he'd been too intoxicated to exercise command.

The second charge, derived from the first, was that he'd been drunk on duty.

The third charge was "breach of arrest and conduct prejudicial to good order and military discipline," after he snubbed Captain Hardee's attempt to put him under arrest that night at the hacienda.

The fourth was derived from the third, that he'd violated the 27th Article of the Articles of War when he broke arrest. The 27th states that, "All officers, of what condition soever, have power to part and quell all quarrels ... and to order officers into arrest ... until their proper superior officers shall be acquainted therewith; and whosoever shall refuse to obey such officer . . . shall be punished at the discretion of a general court martial."

The first witness for the prosecution was Capt. Henry Hopkins Sibley, who saw Captain Thornton, somewhere west of El Lencero, ride off to the left after a Mexican soldier who'd fired his musket, and then return with the man as a prisoner. "I was then struck with his peculiar manner and unusual excitement, and the farther we proceeded in the pursuit the more impressed from his manner and conduct that he was intoxicated."

Having Captain Sibley as a witness to intoxication is rich with irony. He later became a Confederate general and led a (probably hopeless) expedition that attempted to capture Colorado and California and their goldfields for the South and thus turn the Confederacy into a well-funded, continent-spanning world power. He was known during that campaign for self-medicating a "kidney condition," and was typically effective in the mornings and absent in the afternoons. After the expedition collapsed due to a lack of supplies (and a crippling defeat at Glorieta Pass, New Mexico), he had several minor commands in Louisiana and after the war was a mercenary in Egypt. He had drinking problems in both places. (He was also the inventor of the conical twelve-man Sibley tent, an industrial version of the Plains Indian teepee that the US Army adopted just before the Civil War broke out, putting them in mass production. By joining the Confederacy he cut himself off from a tidy fortune in royalties he would otherwise have collected from the US Army.)

Next at the trial a lieutenant named Keans then testified that he rode with Thornton most of the day. While the accused gave proper orders, "his appearance, language, and actions were those of a man intoxicated," Lieutenant Keans said.

Captain Hardee said he saw Captain Thornton arrive at the hacienda that evening. Thornton was "riding out of ranks and had an unsteady position on horseback," he said. Then came the loud, childish argument with a lieutenant who said Thornton should have killed the Mexican soldier rather than taking him prisoner. Hardee intervened.

There are a couple of other witnesses about the argument and the arrest having happened, and then the prosecution rested. For whatever reason, they did not use the childish argument itself as evidence of intoxication, although intoxication surely would have been the simplest explanation for it.

For his defense, Thornton presented six witnesses who said that they saw him sober that day, and that he was a man of long-standing sober habits, but that he tended to get very excited—intoxicated with excitement—when in action.

The witnesses included Assistant Surgeon J. K. Barnes, who said that during the afternoon he gave Thornton a swig from his canteen containing medicinal liquor—but it was not enough to produce intoxication, he insisted. The accused appeared sober otherwise, he testified.

Oddly, no one accused Thornton of having alcohol on his breath. That may be because all the witnesses had likewise received fortification from Assistant Surgeon Barnes that afternoon, and could not smell it on anyone else.

Or, Thornton may actually have been sober.

Thornton spent no time during the trial on the incident with Hardee—rightly so, since a conviction of being drunk on duty or on Article 52 could end his career, whereas a disagreement with Hardee was just a disagreement with Hardee.

The results were announced on June 2, 1847. His careful dance around the concepts of intoxication and excitement worked, as the court found him not guilty of the first two charges, those being the ones related to drunkenness and Article 52. They also found him not guilty of the fourth change, that of violating Article 27.

They convicted him of the third charge, "Breach of arrest and conduct prejudicial to good order and military discipline," except they dropped the words "breach of arrest and." So he was convicted only of "conduct prejudicial to good order and military discipline." He was sentenced to be "reprimanded in official orders."

So, once again, his skills as a barracks lawyer kept him in the army. He probably considered himself lucky. But the end result of staying in the army was that he had seventy-eight days left to live.

By August 7 Scott had massed a mobile force of nearly eleven thousand men. That day he left a small garrison to hold Puebla (population seventy thousand) and set off with the rest of his army toward Mexico City (population two hundred thousand) eighty miles to the west, in the high, swampy, Valley of Mexico.

Towns in the broad Valley of Mexico were connected (as they had been in Aztec times) by elevated causeways. Since they were hard to out-flank through the swamps, fortified points on these causeways were readily defended. The best, most direct road into the city was dominated by a hill that Santa Anna had fortified with great fanfare. After energetic scouting the US force found a good, unobstructed road that led into the southern end of the valley. Going about twenty-five miles out of their way, they emerged August 17 at the town of San Augustin, about nine miles south of Mexico City.

The next town to the north was San Antonio (unrelated to the one in Texas, of course). It was fortified, with cannons covering the road. The next day, August 18, the dragoons went forward to scout its defenses, and the defenders opened fire with their artillery. It was the first Mexican fortification they had probed since Cerro Gordo, and it was firing its first shot at them.

Captain Thornton, on horseback, leading the advance guard from the front, had just gotten into range with his party when the defenders fired that shot. It was an eighteen-pounder, meaning it fired an eighteen-pound cannonball that was about five inches in diameter. It hit him square in the chest, killing him outright. It then hit the road behind him and sprayed rock fragments into the rest of his party, seriously wounding another man.[8]

To pass chest-high to a man on horseback and then immediately hit the ground indicates (assuming level ground) that the cannonball was descending in a fairly steep arc, and so must have been fired at long range for such a gun, roughly fifteen hundred yards.[9]

Hitting a moving, man-size target at extreme range using the methods available to the Mexican gunners (manual manipulation of the carriage, aiming across naked metal gun sights, crude range finders, and gunpowder that was inconsistent from charge to charge) had to have been pure chance.

Clearly, his luck never changed.

"The hardships of that terrible journey [inland to Mexico City] preyed upon his naturally delicate constitution, and rendered him an invalid before the city of Montezuma's greeted the army's longing sight," wrote a frontline journalist. "Eager, however, for duty, nothing would prevail on him to be inactive, as soon as prospect of battle presented. During the reconnaissance near San Antonio, on the evening of the 18th August, he accompanied the men, assisting personally in the most fatiguing duties. While thus engaged, a discharge from a battery within the fort struck him dead from his horse, and wounded a guide."[10]

"Much blame had been attributed to him, and for the result of the Affair he had been placed before court martial," said another obituary. "The finding of the court had almost entirely exonerated him; but the very fact of disaster befalling the troops under his leading, although none doubted the brave devotion with which he encountered danger, had preyed upon his chivalric spirit and increased the ravages of the disease which was wearing out his life. He had evidently but a few more weeks to live, yet he kept in his saddle and failed not in any portion of his duty. He met a soldier's fate with characteristic bravery; indeed, his gallant spirit would have chosen such a lot, had it been possible, rather than to have awaited the natural summons of the final messenger."[11] [It's not clear that he actually had a fatal illness, as opposed to a frail constitution, but it seems unlikely, as his health had been an issue since he was a teenager.]

Seth B. Thornton was thirty-two years old. There is no record that he ever married or had a family.

CHAPTER 9

Thornton's Echo

THE DAY AFTER CAPTAIN THORNTON WAS KILLED, THE US FORCE launched an attack on the forces between it and Mexico City, triggering the misnamed Battle of Contreras (Contreras being several miles away). It was followed the next day (August 20, 1847) with the accurately named Battle of Churubusco. By the end of that day Santa Anna's army was in full retreat, and the US forces had recaptured the two guns lost at Buena Vista/Angostura.

Rather than launch a hot pursuit into the city, General Scott stopped his army, arranged a truce, and tried to open negotiations. He had the usual luck with Santa Anna, and eventually called off the armistice. On the morning of September 8, he launched an attack on an old foundry situated in the Mexican defense line, called Molino del Rey (King's Mill). The area had been reinforced by Santa Anna, and General Scott heard that it was because the Mexicans were surreptitiously melting church bells there into desperately needed cannons. To believe such a thing he must have had no understanding of the industrial requirements of cannon production. Bloody, pointless fighting went on for half a day before they took the building, where they found a few old gun moulds and no newly cast cannons. Scott's army lost about eight hundred men out of a total force of less than ten thousand.

Molino del Rey was adjacent to the grounds of Chapultepec, a wooded park that had been used as a retreat by the Aztec rulers. In the middle was a two-hundred-foot hill topped by Chapultepec Castle, home of the Mexican army's military academy. (The castle itself did not date back to the Aztecs, having been built by the Spanish in 1775.) Its position in the causeway grid left it guarding the main approach to Mexico City from the west, and Scott decided to penetrate the city's defenses at that point. (Unconsciously or otherwise, he may have wanted to justify taking Molino del Rey.)

Despite being called a castle, the building was not designed for defense. After a daylight-hours artillery barrage on September 12, the US forces were able to storm it the next morning, albeit not without drama and more than eight hundred casualties.

"I believe if we were to plant our batteries in hell the damned Yankees would take them from us," Santa Anna supposedly remarked to a bystander on seeing the US flag raised over the castle. "God is a Yankee," the bystander agreed.[1]

Waiting on the other side of the lines were thirty former US soldiers with nooses around their necks, members of the San Patricio Battalion who had defected to the Mexican army. They had been captured by US forces at Churubusco and sentenced to death for deserting to the enemy. As the flag went up they were hanged.

Chapultepec taken, the US forces then stormed down the two causeways linking the park to Mexico City. They were stymied on one but poured into the city on the other. Santa Anna pulled out of the city that night, and the US flag flew over the main plaza the next morning.

The war then wound down. Santa Anna tried to retake Puebla, presumably to form a base for the remnants of his army, and stepped down when that didn't work. A new junta gradually took control and agreed to negotiate. The negotiations ran into many hurdles (Polk at one point recalled his emissary, and the emissary ignored him) but eventually produced the Treaty of Guadalupe Hidalgo. Finalized in May 1848, it added to the United States all or parts of what is now California, Nevada, Utah, Arizona, Kansas, Colorado, Wyoming, Oklahoma, and New Mexico, as well as acknowledging Texas with the Rio Grande as the border. The United States agreed to cover the adjudicated expropriation claims and pay Mexico an additional $15 million in annual payments of $3 million. (The $3 million to "facilitate negotiations" was finally handed over.) The last US troops left the country through Vera Cruz on August 2, 1848.[2]

By then gold fever was raging in newly acquired California. The Trans-Nueces War and Captain Thornton were quickly forgotten. The spot where he was ambushed cannot now even be located (see Chapter 12).

But it can be said that the entire Trans-Nueces remains forgotten. It is now known for high poverty rates and for being the only large metropolitan area in the contiguous United States not reached by the Interstate Highway System.

The Fort Brown earthwork, built to over-awe Matamoros, was abandoned shortly after General Taylor occupied that city. Most of it was obliterated by later levee construction. The southwest corner survived as a serpentine brush-covered mound in what became the northwest corner of the Fort Brown Memorial Golf Course. But then the controversial border fence was built. Although the site remains US territory, it was left on the Mexican side of the fence, being in a bend of the river with Mexico on three sides with the fence crossing the neck of the bend. Business fell off and the golf course closed in 2015.[3]

Fort Brown the military post was established after the war a few hundred yards to the north of the original earthwork, and the city of Brownsville grew up beside it. Decommissioned in 1946, the post has become a college campus.

At Resaca de la Palma, the spot where Capt. Charles May vaulted to fame is now the bridge where Parades Line Road crosses the resaca, which has been dredged and flooded to serve the municipal water system. (The road was named after a local landowner, not the Mexican president at the time of the battle.) The battlefield northwest of the bridge, where most of the fighting took place, is lost under suburban development. A largely vacant thirty-five-acre tract of land just northeast of the bridge, formerly a polo field, was finally acquired by the US National Park Service in 2011.

Aside from improved drainage encouraging the growth of brush, the Palo Alto battlefield has changed little. The Palo Alto Battlefield National Historical Park was established in 1978 and has acquired about sixteen hundred acres of the battlefield.

As for the officious, meddling Maj. Thomas T. Fauntleroy, after ten years as a major he finally got promoted a grade, to lieutenant colonel, in June 1846, about the time Captain Thornton's court-martial was in progress. (He was probably sorry he missed it.) After the war he was made colonel of the 1st Dragoons and served at various posts in California and the West, campaigning with the famous Kit Carson at one point.

He resigned his commission in May 1861, as southern secession was breaking up the nation and the army. He was appointed a brigadier general of the Virginia army. But after it was absorbed into the Confederate army the new hierarchy would not confirm his commission. (Perhaps they knew him too well.) So he quit, resigning as of August 30, 1861.[4] He sat out the war and died in 1883.[5]

As for Bvt. Lt. Col. Charles A. May, he was later promoted to brevet colonel and officially to major, and was still at that rank when he resigned on April 20, 1861, in the midst of the secession crisis. But instead of going south to join the Confederacy, he went north and became the vice president of a streetcar company in New York City. Streetcars were pulled by horses, and as a dragoon officer he was familiar with horse management, so it fit. He had been complaining of an unspecified health problem since 1850, and it claimed him in 1864.[6]

As for 2nd Lt. Elias Kent Kane, who rode with Captain Thornton and was also captured in the Affair, he got promoted to first lieutenant a year later, and to captain and quartermaster a year after that. But he, too, had unspecified health problems, and died in 1853.[7]

Their commander, Col. David Twiggs, rose two grades to brevet major general during the war. He later became commander of the Department of Texas, and there being no retirement plan in the US Army at the time, he was still there, at age seventy, when secession began. A southerner from Georgia, he immediately surrendered the department and all its installations to the Confederacy, was dismissed from the US Army, joined the Confederate army, but then resigned due to bad health, and died of pneumonia in 1862.[8]

Besides having a brother and nephew on the *Pulaski*, he had another brother and nephew who served in the Mexican War, and both were killed there. His younger brother, Maj. Levi Twiggs, USMC, died leading one of the storming parties at Chapultepec. The participation of the US Marine Corps in that action is commemorated in the opening words of the Marines' Hymn, "From the halls of Montezuma. . . ."

His death there took place a month and a day after the death of his nineteen-year-old son, George Decatur Twiggs, who was a volunteer aide-de-camp to the commander of a resupply column moving inland from Vera Cruz. He was killed in a sharp fight against guerrillas at the Puente Nacional, a massive stone bridge between Vera Cruz and Cerro Gordo.[9] Perhaps Major Twiggs would have found comfort in the last lines of the hymn: "If the Army and the Navy/Ever look on Heaven's scenes/They will find the streets are guarded/By United States Marines."

Also at Chapultepec the Mexican government has built a memorial to the six *Niños Héroes* (Boy Heroes), cadets who refused to surrender to the attackers, one of them leaping from the walls with the Mexican flag so the invaders could not get it. The anniversary of the battle, September 13, is now a national holiday.

Meanwhile, the commanders on both sides in the Trans-Nueces War rose to be president of their nations. The low-key Zachary Taylor was embraced by the Whig party, mostly because of his newfound celebrity status, and was elected in 1848. (Polk, a Democrat, did not seek re-election, having run on a promise not to do so, and died three months after leaving office.) Taylor was his own man, and substantially ignored the Whig platform (especially the anti-war rhetoric). A slave-owning southerner, he nevertheless arranged for California to be admitted as a non-slave state. He died of a sudden intestinal ailment on July 9, 1850. The colorless Millard Fillmore then took over.

On the other side, Gen. Mariano Arista was dismissed from command for losing Matamoros, but that didn't stop him from becoming president of Mexico in 1851. He fought for fiscal stability but turned out to be too liberal and fled into exile after two years, dying at sea in 1855.[10]

Santa Anna, stripped of his offices, went into exile again in May 1848, again passing with permission through the US lines. As usual he made a comeback, returning to power in April 1853. After about two years he was overthrown for good, after selling more of Mexico to the United States in the Gadsden Purchase in 1854, and also declaring himself dictator for life with the title of Most Serene Highness. His final exile (during which he helped found the chewing gum industry) lasted twenty-one years. His second wife stayed loyal. When they were back in

Mexico, when she saw he was depressed, she would go into the street and get people to come in and talk to him and hear stories about the old days. His end came in 1876.[11]

As for the man who drove him out of Mexico City, Gen. Winfield Scott turned down an offer to be made dictator of Mexico and returned to the United States to become the commanding general of the US Army. His celebrity status caused the Whigs to nominate him for the 1852 presidential election, but he was defeated by Franklin Pierce. Scott thereafter got into a series of feuds with Pierce's secretary of war, Jefferson Davis, and would not consider following him south during the secession crisis. Instead he developed a plan for Union conquest of the Confederacy, called the Anaconda Plan. He also arranged for the engineering officer who had been his right-hand man in Mexico, Robert E. Lee, to replace him as commanding general, but he did not get the response he expected from Lee. He retired anyway, and lived to see his plan eventually carried out before dying in 1866.

And then there was Capt. William Joseph Hardee, second in command during the Affair, who happily blamed everything on Captain Thornton when he thought his commander was dead. He survived the war with his reputation more or less intact, rising to brevet lieutenant colonel. But all that became noise when his wife began dying of tuberculosis in 1851, and he started taking extensive leaves of absence. She passed on June 10, 1853, leaving him with three girls and a boy. He was then called to Washington for an unexpected assignment. As the graduate of a French military school, he was to translate and adapt the latest French drill manuals for use in the US Army. After fighting riflemen in Algeria, the French forces had abandoned their previous emphasis on mass and precision in favor of speed and flexibility.

The resulting "Hardee's Rifle and Light Infantry Tactics" brought him wide professional recognition after its adoption in 1856, despite jealous rumors that it was just a translation. (Parts were, but other parts were not, as the French and US armies had different regimental organizations and command responsibilities.) "Tactics" referred to the canned drills (called evolutions) that a commander could combine to rapidly bring his men into formations that concentrated firepower on the enemy from their single-shot rifles. After more duty on the frontier, he was called to West Point in 1856 as commandant of cadets, staying in that high-profile job to 1860, eventually rising to (non-brevet) lieutenant colonel.

He went south during the secession crisis and eventually became a corps commander in the Army of Tennessee in the Confederacy's western theater. Lacking the unquestioned leadership provided by Gen. Robert E. Lee in the eastern theater, high command in the west was a snake pit of feuds, jealousies, and petty politics that Hardee found distasteful, especially after he remarried well. He ended up turning down command of the army after it was offered to him following the removal of Gen. Braxton Bragg after its stunning defeat at Missionary Ridge. (That was the same Bragg who had served as Captain Thornton's co-counsel.)

Initially, the Hardee tactical system was heavily used by both sides, and provided important advantages for units that were able to master it after weeks of drill and practice. But trench warfare and repeating rifles gradually prevailed, so that only two evolutions finally mattered—somehow get there alive, and dig in.

He surrendered with the Army of Tennessee on April 26, 1865—about four weeks after the death of his sixteen-year-old son, who had been mortally wounded while also serving in the Army of Tennessee. He settled at his second wife's estates in the vicinity of Demopolis, Alabama, west of Selma. In the postwar years he was involved in various business projects, some successful, some not. Finally, his finicky eating habits took on new meaning when he was diagnosed with stomach cancer. No real treatment was available. He fought it for six months. His third and final surrender came on November 6, 1873.[12] He was fifty-eight.

Probably unknown to him, his postwar home was about twenty-five miles east of Captain Thornton's final resting place in the Myrtle Cemetery in Livingston, Alabama. Thornton's sister described it as the family burial ground, and other Thorntons are buried there, including his older brother, Henry Randolph Thornton, who died in 1862. She said that Bvt. Maj. Gen. William J. Worth (a division commander in General Scott's army) handled the removal of the remains from Mexico. Reburial took place in March 1848.

After more than a century and a half the marker remains legible, bravely trying to sum up a man's life on a small slab of stone. As was his practice in life, his middle name wasn't spelled out:

SETH B. THORNTON
Captain, 2nd. Dragoons, U.S.A.
born in Orange county, Va
May 28th, 1815
killed in Mexico, in the
service of his Country
August 18th, 1847

Dulce et decorum est pro patria mori

The last line, of course, is from the Roman poet Horace, often used with military monuments: "It is sweet and glorious to die for one's country."

CHAPTER 10

The Bigger Echo

In July 1986—140 years and three months after the Thornton Affair—an emissary of Mexican president Miguel de la Madrid met with opposition leaders about the results of the gubernatorial election in Chihuahua.[1] Embarrassingly, the candidate of Madrid's incumbent party, the PRI (*Partido Revolucionario Institucional*, the Institutional Revolutionary Party) had lost. The candidate of the nascent opposition party, PAN (*Partido Acción Nacional*, the National Action Party) had apparently been elected by a three-to-one margin. Despite running Mexico as a one-party state since 1929, and despite having the power of the government covertly (or even overtly) behind it to crush opposition, the PRI had lost an election. Some would say that democracy had triumphed.

Instead of that happening, the emissary explained that the election would not be allowed to go to the victorious PAN candidate. If a governor was in power who was not a member of the ruling party, the sovereignty of Mexico would be undermined by a conspiracy led by the United States. The opposition leaders did not share his views, but could not shake the emissary. "Electoral alchemy" then added another link to a chain of Mexican political paranoia whose origins can be traced to 1846. (It has since weakened enough to allow opposition victories.)

That an unlucky, sickly, stubborn, and moderately paranoid US Army officer should have injected stubborn paranoia into the Mexican political culture is, of course, saying too much. The contribution of Seth B. Thornton was just one thread in the complex tapestry of Mexican history. But it may be an important thread.

For three centuries prior to independence, Mexico had been kept weak and fragmented so it could be readily exploited by the Spanish crown. A generation after independence, in 1846, Mexico was still weak and fragmented, and Santa Anna was making an off-and-on career out of exploiting it. The United States found it was also able to exploit it, acquiring territory that Mexico proved unable to defend. Had the United States not done so, someone else almost certainly would have.

And indeed, less than a generation later France tried to do much the same thing, installing an Austrian prince as its puppet Mexican monarch. But things had changed. Despite invading with better than three times more men than General Scott ever had, it took the French a year and a half to reach Mexico City. They lost large-scale battles to the Mexicans, something that never happened with the US invaders. After the end of the US Civil War in 1865, the French found they had an additional enemy poised on the Rio Grande, withdrew, and their puppet prince died in front of a Mexican firing squad in 1867.

After some more turmoil, the ascendance of a new dictator, Porfirio Diaz, provided a form of stability until his fall in 1911. Turmoil followed, with some more cases of foreign (i.e., US) intervention. The biggest (the pursuit of Pancho Villa in 1916) rivaled General Scott's invasion in size. In the end national sovereignty prevailed with the PRI eventually providing a form of stability. At this writing a multi-party system appears to be functioning, while it is the turn of drug cartels to promote weakness and fragmentation. History will not be on their side.

The dilemma of both individuals and nations is that good decisions are the product of experience, and experience is the product of bad decisions. Both the United States and Mexico have had enough mutual experience that there is no further excuse for bad decisions. Through his enablement of a monumental example of mutual experience, Seth Brett Thornton may have served both countries equally well.

CHAPTER 11

What If...

Captain Thornton submitted a written summation at his court-martial, which noted the following (included in the attachment at the end of Appendix E):

I contend then that the result of my expedition was not disastrous. Nearly half of a squadron of Dragoons were captured, I admit; but what signifies that when compared with the immense advantage to a Commanding General, of knowing his real position, of being confident he no longer occupied debatable ground, of being certain the enemy were gaining his rear in force and determined to give him battle. If this was not important information, why the immediate requisition for heavy re-inforcements? Why the redoubled activity in the completion of Fort Brown? Why the sudden and rapid move upon Point Isabel for ammunition and provisions?

But for the loss of this squadron, gentlemen, for which I am called on to atone, the thanks of a grateful people might never have been tendered to the "Heroes of Palo Alto and Resaca de la Palma." But, instead of tears of destitute widows and the cries of helpless orphans might have been answered as they heretofore been with cold indifference in the halls of our National legislature. Rather than such should be the case I would willingly conceal in my breast again, however painful and difficult the task, the only bleeding heart amidst the rejoicing of a victorious army.

In other words, "You should be glad I ran into that Mexican force. It was unlucky for me, but the rest of the army was alerted to the danger facing it and was able to respond appropriately and save itself. The alternative could have been a bloody defeat."

Of course, there was more to it than that. The primary thing that General Taylor learned from the Thornton Affair was that the Mexicans would fight. That changed everything.

Digging in under the shadow of Matamoros's defenses, outnumbered five to three, two-days' march from any support they could get from their port along a road they could not protect, with no flank protection at all, made sense only as a theatrical display of military power intended to give the Mexican government an excuse to cave in to Polk's graduated pressure. The Mexican politicians could show the Mexican public that they had been coerced and their only recourse was to take the US money. Large sums would change hands, the border would change, and rational people would be happy.

That wasn't going to happen, General Taylor must have realized when he learned of the Affair. The Mexican army would have to be defeated—and he was off to a poor start, since a large Mexican cavalry force was now in his rear, and there was little he could do about it. He did not have anywhere near enough mounted troops to defeat it, and it could simply avoid his infantry force. So it could just lurk out there, its horses feeding off the plentiful grass, keeping Taylor cut off from his base.

On the plus side he did have the almost finished fort, which was too strong for the Mexicans to attack. It could be used as a base for further operations if he could secure access to it. But securing access would have required miles of trenches and outposts, both along the river and inland, to protect the road back to the port. They would have to be manned by more soldiers than the US Army possessed.

And so he rushed the completion of the fort and sent out an appeal for state militia reinforcements—i.e., half-trained infantry that could not be counted on to press attacks on a battlefield, but could be counted on to patrol a riverbank and defend their outposts. As soon as the fort was finished, General Taylor sent his wagon train back to Port Isabel guarded by most of his force, leaving just enough troops in the fort to hold it.

General Arista, having concentrated his force on the north side of the river, left a force to besiege the fort and placed the rest of his army in position to strike the US force when it returned. That way he could fight a decisive battle before his own ill-supplied force fell apart from hunger. When General Taylor's force did reappear again on the road from the north, Arista struck at it. Up to that point, his plan worked. But during the subsequent dual battles of Palo Alto and Resaca de la Palma, he was crushed.

Had Captain Thornton been less stubborn and turned back when Chipito said he should have, there would have been no confirmation of Mexican intentions, or of the presence of a large Mexican force in the rear of the US force. Taylor could have decided the whole thing was another rumor. The appearance of General Torrejon's force astride the road to Port Isabel would have been a complete surprise. Worse yet, he might not have noticed it until the rest of the Mexican army crossed downstream and converged on the fort.

The US force would then have been isolated and besieged. General Taylor only had a few days' supply for his whole force in the fort,[1] so moving most of it back to the port (where it could be fed by sea from New Orleans) was essential. But that meant fighting his way back to Point Isabel, with the enemy to the front and rear. Assuming he could have kept his army organized as it retreated he could probably have fought off Arista's infantry, but protecting his three-mile-long wagon train from the cavalry would have been difficult. His army could have become strung out, with parts out of range of their artillery cover, so that the Mexicans could have closed in and used their numerical advantage.

If General Arista had any luck pressing the US force as it retreated, many more US soldiers might have ended up surrendering and joining Captain Thornton as prisoners. Those who got to the Point Isabel fortifications (probably by abandoning the wagon train) would have been safe, if only because they could evacuate by sea.

Assuming Taylor's force made it back to Point Isabel largely intact, the campaign would then have stalemated. Taylor would not have had a wagon train to feed his army during any maneuvering it might attempt, and Arista would not have been able to take or besiege the port.

The US Congress would not have declared war after getting news of the Thornton Affair, since there would have been no Affair. Likely, President Polk would have presented his case for war on the basis of the failure of Slidell's mission—just as a series of reports about the increasingly dire situation of General Taylor's army began arriving. Presumably Congress would still have declared war, but the mood would have changed as more and more bad news arrived. The focus of the subsequent campaign would probably have been to rescue Taylor's army and prevent incursions into Texas. The political capital needed to support a larger war, to push the US border to the Pacific Ocean, might not have been there.

If the worst had happened, Taylor had suffered a complete disaster because there was no Thornton Affair, and the bulk of the US Army was destroyed outside Matamoros, the expansionists might have been discredited and there would have been no serious talk of Manifest Destiny. The United States would not have spread to the Pacific Ocean and would not have dominated North America. The region could have become a snake pit of smaller, competing nation-states, not capable of countering the totalitarian ideologies that dominated parts of Europe and Asia during the next century.

On the other hand, the acquisition of Oregon might have taken place anyway. California might well have fallen to a Texas-like secessionist movement by US settlers, and been annexed by the United States. US business interests in the territory between Texas and California might have become so dominant that the inhabitants would have become prone to pro–US revolutions like the one in 1898 in Hawaii, especially if Mexico continued to be unable to protect them from Comanche raids. Or, considering Santa Anna's willingness to sign over parts of Mexico for cash (as in the Gadsden Purchase in 1853) other deals might have been possible.

The United States might still have ended up with borders (and influence on the world stage) reminiscent of what it has today, without

Mexico having acquired the same tradition of victimization by its neighbor to the north.

Of course, we can't run the experiment. We'll never know what would have happened if Capt. Seth B. Thornton hadn't been so stubborn. But, obviously, there are many ways the war could have ended differently, diverging from that moment he made his decision to press on to Las Rusias.

CHAPTER 12

The Affair's Location

In late 1847 freshman Illinois congressman Abraham Lincoln, an anti-administration Whig, tried to force the Democratic Polk Administration to prove that the site of the Thornton Affair had actually been on American soil, and therefore justify the war. (Presumably, he assumed the Democrats would face embarrassment when they couldn't prove it.) He was ignored—and that's a pity, since presenting proof would have involved identifying the site.

Basically, thanks to the ceaseless meandering of the Rio Grande we really can't pinpoint the site today—although, as shown below, we can make some educated guesses. Admittedly, the previous statement flies in the face of the fact that, in 1936, the State of Texas erected a roadside historical marker for the Thornton Affair, on the north side of US 281, just east of where it crosses Cannon Road, two miles west of downtown Los Indios, Texas (population approximately one thousand). Surrounded by treeless farm fields, it adjoins a picnic area with about six trees, a parking strip, and no facilities. The name of the cross street doubtless refers to the presence of a muzzle-loading cannon mounted in concrete beside the marker, pointing toward Mexico. It was placed there by a local chapter of the National Society of the Daughters of the American Revolution.[1]

The state marker itself is inscribed with the words, HERE CAPTAIN PHILIP THORNTON AND 62 DRAGOONS WERE ATTACKED BY MEXICAN TROOPS.[2]

There are several problems with this marker: Who's Philip Thornton? There weren't sixty-two dragoons, although the count is apparently from

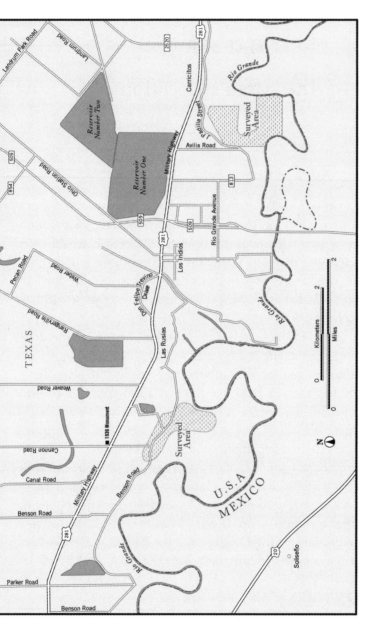

This modern map of the border in the vicinity of Los Indios, Texas, shows the two areas surveyed by US government archaeologists in the 1990s in an unsuccessful search for the site of the Thornton Affair. If modern Las Rusias is the same as the 1846 Las Rusias, the Affair likely happened either in the Carricitos area, or in the middle of Los Indios near the intersection of FM 509 and US 281, but all proposed identifications have problems. Modern Soliseño, in the lower left, is the same as the 1846 Soliseño. Credit: Alena Pearse the regiment's first historian[3] who, relying on initial estimates, listed nine dead, four wounded, and forty-nine missing (i.e., captured). Most especially, the Affair clearly happened on the north bank of the Rio Grande, but the marker is not even in sight of the river, which is located not quite a mile to the south of the marker and hidden from it by rolls in the ground. Of course, that could be accounted for by the river's meanderings since 1846, but you'd expect it to have left a resaca. Aerial photos show several in the area, but none closer than half a mile—and to the north.[4]

In 1997 the National Park Service published[5] the results of several scientific attempts to locate the site of the Affair—and announced that it had failed. They surveyed two likely areas, and found some evidence of mid-nineteenth-century occupation—and of a lot of plowing and levee construction. They found no military artifacts from 1846, or any topography that matched the maps presented at the two trials. The report cites a local legend that the skirmish took place in the area between the 1936 marker and the river—and that legend presumably explains how the marker got there. (Or, perhaps the marker sparked the legend.) So they surveyed the area, but no evidence surfaced of military activity.

They also surveyed the area between Carricitos and the river. Carricitos is the name for an old neighborhood on the eastern side of Los Indios, just west of the intersection of US 281 and Farm Road 2520,[6] six miles east of the monument. Since the site of the Affair is often given as Rancho de Carricitos, it's not hard to imagine a connection, but again the archaeologists found nothing.

But if modern place names can be a clue, we have the fact that the patrol was on its way to a place called Las Rusias, and never got there. According to the *Handbook of Texas*,[7] Las Rusias is now a neighborhood on the east side of Los Indios, near the intersection of US 281 and Rangerville Road. Google Maps puts it at the same intersection, which is two miles east of the monument and three miles west of Carricitos.

Could modern Las Rusias be the same as the 1846 Las Rusias? Maybe so. A 1903 Boundary Commission[8] map shows the river's course as surveyed in 1898 and in 1853. The two courses often diverge widely, giving no clue as to the river's course in 1846. None of it resembles the topography shown in the hand-drawn maps used in the trials. But the

1898 survey shows a ranch on the north side of the river called Las Rusias. Plotting longitude and latitude places it within a hundred yards of the modern location. The locale is also cited as the Las Rusias where a Civil War skirmish took place in 1864. So assuming the name was also used for the vicinity in 1846 does not seem unreasonable.

Assuming we have found Las Rusias, the 1936 monument cannot be correct, as it is located two miles west of Las Rusias, and the patrol, coming from the east, never got as far west as Las Rusias except as prisoners. But how close to Las Rusias did they get?

The specifications at Thornton's court-martial say the Affair happened "near" Las Rusias. Thornton's report, written two days after the Affair and while he was still a prisoner of war, said his guide left him while the patrol was three miles from the goal (which he rendered as "La Rusia" or "La Rosia") and the ambush happened two miles later, placing the Affair one mile from Las Rusias. That would place the Affair inside modern Los Indios, about where the road to the international bridge intersects US 281. While it may seem odd that Thornton knew how far he was from Las Rusias at the time, as he had not reached that point yet and had never been there before, he probably went through it as a prisoner later, as his captors retraced the route they took from Matamoros.

Captain Hardee, in his testimony in the Thornton court-martial, called the site "Las Rosies," and said the Affair happened three miles short of it. (He, too, would have covered the distance as a prisoner.) Assuming he had the distance right (and he got many things wrong) that puts the Affair in modern Carricitos, giving the name association more weight.

Meanwhile, there are the sketch maps. The one submitted during the Thornton court-martial shows a road leaving the western end of the plantation labeled "road to Las Rusias," with no indication of how far it was to Las Rusias. The map submitted with the court of inquiry shows that the distance between the western end of the plantation and Las Rusias was about one-ninth the distance from Las Rusias to Matamoros, which is given elsewhere as twenty-seven miles. That would put the Affair three miles from Las Rusias, as Captain Hardee stated—but the map is not otherwise drawn to scale.

Finally, the modern configuration of Don Felipe Trevino Drive on the western side of Los Indios would seem to match the layout of the plantation in the court-martial map, especially if US 281 is taken to match the approximate course of the river in 1846. There is even a rectangular pond that matches the shape and placement of the morass in the sketch map, and Weber Road appears to match the trail into the prairie that the patrol followed for a few minutes before turning back to the river road. If these features are indeed survivors of the layout of the plantation, the Affair took place in what was at this writing the parking lot of a trucking company. But modern Las Rusias is immediately to the west of that parking lot, so it must be assumed that both Captains Thornton and Hardee got the distance to Las Rusias wrong, or that the site name drifted to the east (or both). But there is another problem with the site: The area between Don Felipe Trevino Drive and US 281, resembling the plantation in the sketch map, is about sixty acres. Captain Hardee, testifying in the Thornton court-martial, estimated that the plantation covered three hundred acres. Assuming his estimate had any validity, the dimensions of the modern features would have to be about double what they are to enclose that much space. But that can be at least partially accomplished by moving the presumed location of the river farther to the south.

Assuming that Captains Thornton and Hardee were at least vaguely correct, and that the 1846 Las Rusias and the modern Las Rusias are in the same neighborhood, then the Affair must have happened inside what is now Los Indios, possibly as far east as the Carricitos neighborhood. But considering that the participants were exhausted, then scrambling for their lives, and then reeling in shock, there's little reason to assume total accuracy, and the parking lot cannot be ruled out.

It's also entirely possible that the river's meandering has left the site (the violation of which caused the United States to go to war) on the Mexican side of the river. Lincoln would have relished the irony.

APPENDIXES

APPENDIX A

The US Army in Early 1846

Overview

While the units were at about 40 percent strength due to peacetime budget limitations, they were otherwise clothed, armed, supplied, and trained to the best affordable standards.

Strength

There were 7,365 soldiers, organized in eight infantry, two dragoon, and four artillery regiments. All were under-strength because the 1842 retrenchment was still in force, with fifty privates per company in the dragoons and forty-two in the other arms. Bringing them up to the standard strength of one hundred would require a months-long process of recruitment and training. For immediate reinforcement it was possible to mobilize state militia units of varying quality, but they depended on the regular army for supplies. The regulars saw them as something of a plague.

Command Structure

The regular army was well organized and well trained. But most units were in small frontier garrisons and, as noted, retained peacetime strength levels. There was also a general shortage of officers. There had been no large-formation fighting since the War of 1812, so the officers had little experience managing or maneuvering formations above the company level. Aside from the Texas Rangers, no militia or volunteer units were involved in the Trans-Nueces fighting, although many participated in subsequent phases of the war.

The army dealt with the officer shortage with the so-called brevet system, in which officers were given brevet ranks appropriate for their assignments in the absence of official promotions approved by Congress. They continued to receive pay and seniority-based promotions according to their official rank. For instance, Bvt. Brig. Gen. Zachary Taylor, commander of the Army of Observation, was officially a colonel. Officially, there were only three generals in the army when the war started.

While individual officers might be active in politics, as a social institution the US Army was not a player in national politics.

Arms

The infantry used a late-model smoothbore flintlock musket, maintained by specialists. A percussion smoothbore musket (which would have been more reliable, although no more accurate) had been adopted but had not yet reached the troops. The dragoons carried a variety of weapons, some deceptively modern.

The artillery had been recently modernized, but still suffered (compared to modern guns) from the use of black powder and the lack of recoil absorbing mechanisms. The former meant inconsistent muzzle velocities from one shot to the next, so that range was not entirely predictable. The latter meant that the cannon had to be allowed to roll backward with each shot to absorb the recoil, then pushed back into position and re-aimed. Also, the gun could only be elevated a limited amount, restricting the possible range. Otherwise the recoil could smash the wooden carriage.

Ammunition

The gunpowder was scientifically formulated and manufactured, and exceeded government specifications. But being black powder (charcoal, sulfur, and potassium nitrate) it was about one-fifth the power of modern nitrocellulose. It could produce enough smoke to screen troop movements. Exploding shells broke into large pieces, sometimes leaving nearby bystanders unhurt. But US Army bullets were mass-produced and identical, and invariably fit the guns.

Logistics

Long-service specialists in adequately funded departments with tight financial controls saw to the army's needs. Shortages of any description triggered scandals.

Steamboats and especially railroads were still in their infancy, so the army often had to rely on traditional columns of horse-drawn wagon trains for resupply. Since the animals pulling the wagons would eat the contents of the wagons after about thirteen days, major maneuvers required that the army eventually live off the land. The US Army in Mexico did this successfully by paying cash for all supplies, even as unfunded enemy formations in the same region starved, descended into brigandage, or disintegrated.

APPENDIX B

El Ejército Mexicano en 1846

Overview

On paper, the Mexican army was several times larger than the US Army, and its soldiers were paid about twice as much. In reality it was a façade that could do little but prop up local warlords. However, its limitations never prevented the Mexican soldiers from fighting.

Strength

There were 18,882 regulars, organized into twelve infantry regiments, eight cavalry regiments plus one independent squadron, three artillery brigades, five companies of field artillery, one dragoon brigade, and one battalion of engineers. Plus there were 10,495 "active militia" organized in nine infantry and six cavalry regiments. (The distinction between regulars and active militia was dropped in 1849.) On paper there were another 1,174 "presidial" troops (frontier fort garrisons).[1]

Command Structure

The destructive ten-year War of Independence that ended in 1821 had left a political culture based on regional *caudillos* (warlords). Most of the troops were in scattered garrisons that propped up local warlords, with no consideration for national security, leaving the army largely ineffective against ongoing threats like the Comanches and Apaches. Pay rarely arrived and military service was considered an undesirable alternative to incarceration, even though soldiers were immune to civilian courts. (Some infantry units were actually convicts in chain gangs.) The warlords liked to hand out commissions to their friends, or sell them for revenue, and so (on the rolls anyway) officers often outnumbered enlisted soldiers.

Arms

The infantry mostly carried the "Morena Licha" (Dark Alice), i.e., the Brown Bess smoothbore flintlock musket, a Napoleonic War relic purchased from the British government. Age and the lack of expert maintenance had not improved these firearms, which had been hastily manufactured under wartime conditions to begin with. But they could still hold a bayonet.

Firearms training would have required the expenditure of expensive ammunition, and so was unknown.

The field artillery pieces were relics inherited from the Spanish, produced with the so-called Gribeauval technology dating to the 1760s. Otherwise comments about the US artillery also apply.

Ammunition

The gunpowder was actually blasting powder, heavy on cheap charcoal and sulfur and light on expensive potassium nitrate.[2] An infantryman could either watch his bullets bounce off the enemy or use so much powder that his barrel fouled almost immediately. Bullets were made by hand and did not always fit.

The field artillery only fired solid shot but the siege artillery had exploding shells as well. Some cannonballs were copper, which worked as well as the iron ones.

Logistics

There was no commissary system. Money for supplies, when available, was simply handed out to the *soldaderas* (women who attached themselves to the army), who bought and prepared food. (Otherwise they raised chickens and vegetables.) The system worked in garrison towns, but when a unit had to move any distance all supply arrangements had to be extemporized and the results could resemble a death march.

APPENDIX C

Order of Battle, US and Mexican Forces, Trans-Nueces War

These charts shows the organization and strength of the US and Mexican forces at the start of the Battle of Palo Alto.[1] The strength of the 2nd Dragoons reflects the loss of fifty-five troopers in the Thornton Affair. The Texas Ranger party had also lost eleven men to the same Mexican force.

US Army, Army of Observation, May 8, 1846
Bvt. Brig. Gen. (Col.) Zachary Taylor

		Soldiers	
Staffs		16	
Right Wing*	3rd Brigade (3rd & 4th Inf. Rgts.)	656	included 2nd Lt. U.S. Grant
	Ringgold's Artillery	54	eight 6-pounders
	2nd Dragoon Rgt.	260	mounted
	5th Inf. Rgt.	378	
1st Brigade	Lt. Inf. Battalion	445	artillerymen used as infantry
	Duncan's Artillery	52	two 18-pounders
	8th Inf. Rgt.	404	
Texas Rangers		25	
Supply train		?	270 wagons
future Fort Brown	Staffs	6	had supplies for two weeks
	7th Inf. Rgt.	428	Approximate
	3 artillery batteries	107	Approximate
Fort Polk (Point Isabel)		400	Approximate

*The army had marched from Corpus Christi as three brigades, but Taylor reorganized when leaving the fort, garrisoning it with units from the 2nd and 3rd Brigades and then merging the 2nd into the 3rd.

Rgt.=Regiment
Lt.=Light
Inf.=Infantry
# pounder=weight of the cannonball fired by a given artillery piece

Ejército Mexicano, División Norte, May 8, 1846
Gen. Mariano Arista

		Soldiers	
Staffs		36	
1st Brigade	Sapper Batt.	346	engineers
	2nd Lt. Inf. Rgt.	356	
	Tampico CG Batt.	146	coastal guards
	Tamaulipas Co.	77	
	artillery units	88	two 8-pounders, six 4-pounders
2nd Brigade	Frontier Auxiliaries	333	
	4th Inf. Rgt.	521	
	Sapper Co.	51	engineers
Inf. Brigade	1st Inf. Rgt.	294	
	6th Inf. Rgt.	209	
	10th Inf. Rgt.	296	
Cav. Brigade	Lt. Cav. Rgt.	227	
	7th Cav. Rgt.	287	
	8th Cav. Rgt.	293	
	1st Cav. Rgt.	40	
	Presidial Co.	134	frontiersmen
Matamoros garrison		1,400	Estimate

Lt.=light
Inf.=infantry
Rgt.=regiment
Co.=company
Batt.=battalion
Cav.=cavalry
# pounder=weight of the cannonball fired by a given artillery piece

APPENDIX D

Transcript: Court of Inquiry, Capt. W. J. Hardee, Matamoros, Mexico, May 1846

What follows is a typescript of the National Archives file of the court of inquiry that Captain Hardee demanded when, basically, he realized that people were saying hurtful things about his role in the Thornton Affair.

As was also the case with the Thornton court-martial trial (see Appendix E), the text was originally written on both sides of the page in ink, and the ink often ran, bled through, or both. Additionally the pages were often frayed and faded along the edges. Some of the handwriting was not expert. Consequently not all the text could be recovered. Text in <angle brackets> are words that the author could not clearly read but could surmise. <Illegible> indicates words the author could not even surmise. However, such gaps rarely destroy the meaning of a passage.

For legibility, ampersands were rendered as "and" plus some abbreviations were made consistent. Otherwise the typescript attempts to match the text and formatting (although not the line breaks or page breaks) of the original file. Aside from section headers, the use of underlining was rare and some "underlining" turned out to be bleed-throughs, and is dispensed with here.

Supporting documents in the original file were in random sequence. They appear here according to alphabetical markings used in the trial:

/A/ Hand-drawn map.
/B/ Hardee's report of April 26, 1846.
/C/ Hardee's opening statement.
/D/ Thornton's report of April 27, 1846.
/E/ Hardee's defense summation.

The hand-drawn "map" is more of a schematic than a map, as it was clearly not drawn to scale.

Transcript text follows:

Proceedings of a Court of Inquiry, held at the Camp of the 5th Regt. U.S. Infantry, in Matamoros, Mexico, by virtue of the following order, vis:

Hd. Quarters, Army of Occupation,
Matamoros, May 20, 1846
Order No. 66

At the request of Capt. W. J. Hardee, 2d Dragoons, a Court of Inquiry is hereby instituted to examine into the nature of certain imputations affecting his character as connected with his conduct in the engagement between Capt. Thornton's command and the Mexicans on the 25th ultimo, and also to examine and <inquire> upon certain statements contained in his official report of said engagement.

> The court will be composed of
>
> | | |
> |---|---|
> | Major T. Staniford, | 5th Infantry |
> | Capt. C. F. Smith, | 2d Artillery |
> | Capt. Wm. Chapman, | 5th Infantry |
> | 1st Lt. W. H. Churchill, | 3d Artillery, Recorder |

and will report a state of facts and its opinion in the case.

The court will meet at 10 o'clock tomorrow in the camp of the 5th Infantry, at a place to be designated by the president.

By Order of Brig. Gen. Taylor
(Signed) WM Bliss
Asst. Adjt. Gen.

Camp of the 5th Infantry
May 26th, 1846

The court met pursuant to the above order

<u>Present</u>

1. Major T. Staniford, 5th Infantry
2. Capt. C. F. Smith, 2d Artillery
3. Capt. W. Chapman, 5th Infantry
Lt. W. H. Churchill, 3d Arty, Recorder

Capt. W. J. Hardee, 2d Dragoons, being called into the court, and having heard the order read, was asked if he had any objection to any of the members named in the order, to which he replied in the negative.

The court was then duly sworn in his presence. Capt. Hardee submitted the paper appended marked C.

Lieut. E. K. Kane, 2d Dragoons, a witness on the part of Capt. Hardee, being duly sworn, says, On the night of the 24th of April, 1846, a squadron of the 2d Dragoons under Capt. Thornton, left the camp of the Army Opposite Matamoros. At the time I knew not where they were going or what their purpose was, and only that they were going up the river. The squadron moved up the river fifteen or sixteen miles and went into a yard and encamped until daylight. They then left and proceeded on up the river. We heard, from this place <and along>, from different persons, contradictory statements in regards to the Mexicans. Some would say that they had crossed, and others that they had not. When we arrived within about three miles of the place where the action occurred we were informed that the Mexicans had crossed in large numbers, and our guide refused to go any farther with us. He stated that the road we would have to go through was very narrow, and that it would be impossible to retreat if we met the Mexicans, or words to that effect, wishing to convey that idea. The advanced guard was then increased to <ten> men, Lt. Mason being placed in command of it, and ordered to keep about a quarter of a mile ahead, if they saw the Mexicans to return immediately upon the squadron, and if they were in <illegible> to fire upon them and retire. The squadron then moved in this order for about three miles. The Mexicans who informed us that the enemy had crossed said it was only about a mile and a half distant to where we would meet them. When we had arrived at the three mile place we came to a large field, or small fields each <open> together. The plan submitted (appended, marked A) presents a correct sketch of the field. After we had marched around the field some distance we made a counter-march, and the squadron was halted at the lower extremity of the field, in the path (marked A). Capt. Thornton, with the advanced guard, left the squadron, and followed the field around, in the direction of the river. He came back and said that he could see several <miles> up and down the river but discovered nothing, and that he would go around to the back (here marked C) and get in the field in that direction. We moved a short distance in the direction of the bars when it was reported by Srgt. Clark, I believe, that he had seen a Mexican entering a small path that ran into the chaparral. The squadron was again halted and Capt. Thornton went himself and examined the path. When he returned he remarked to me that the trail appeared to have been passed through by about <500> horsemen, or words to that effect. He then immediately moved the squadron down the path about a mile, or a mile and a half, and came to a small marshy prairie. He then returned to the <field> at the road. The command moved on and came up with the advanced guard at the bars, which was halted there. Capt. Thornton himself was in the field about 100 yards, and there were some Mexicans running away from a house in the field about 200 yards from the bars. Capt. Thornton turned around in his saddle and made a motion to advance. The squadron advanced, some running, some trotting, some galloping, as I thought, to catch the men who were running away. We got up to the houses, and the men scattered themselves around, examining the houses, and some getting water at the river. Capt. Thornton, with two or three men, was questioning a Mexican. About this <moment> Srgt. Tredo called out to me "There the Mexicans come." Capt. Thornton immediately rode around, and gave the command charge. It was immediately obeyed, excepting by those who were on foot. As soon as we came within 20 or 30 yards of the infantry, Captain Thornton turned around in his saddle to look after the men, who were about 30 yards behind him. At that time the enemy was firing scattering shot. As soon as the squadron came up to Capt. Thornton, they opened a volley of musketry, which made the horses turn to the right. Capt. Thornton remained in front of the enemy during this time. The men were making for the field some 40 yards on the left flank of the infantry. As soon as I got there Capt. Thornton rode up to me and ordered the men to halt and pull the fence down, which the men did not obey as their horses were running away with them. During this time the enemy was about 30 yards on the opposite side of the fence, and they kept up a constant fire. I did not see Capt. Thornton after he gave the order to pull down the fence, until we had gotten over <illegible> of the cross fences running perpendicular to the main fence, when he ran against me, and knocked myself and my horse down. His horse was running away and he could not manage him at all. There were some 6 or 7 men following Capt. Thornton. A few moments after I saw Capt. Hardee, leading some 20 or 30 men, on the same path Capt. Thornton was on. He pulled up his horse and asked me if I was hurt. I was then in the act of getting on a loose horse. I had caught a company horse. His <mare> ran over me and prevented my mounting. This was the 2d horse I had attempted to mount, but the men ran over me both times. I then jumped over the chaparral fence, and ran into the open field for a short distance. To my left I saw Capt. Hardee some distance going in the direction of the river with his men. Knowing that I could not keep up with the squadron, and hearing the enemy's cavalry coming, I ran to the bushes and concealed myself. In about half an hour one of their chain-gang came around and found me.

Question by Capt. Hardee. In what order, and with what front, were the bars passed?

Answer. In single file.

Question by Capt. H. How far was the advanced guard in advance of the main body?

A. They were both together. The advanced was in front but the squadron was closed up upon it, excepting a few men who became separated, in consequence of the <condition> of their hoses, I suppose, after the command was given to advance.

Question by Capt. H. When the squadron entered the field, was any guard placed on the road in front, any sentinel at the bars, or any other precaution taken to prevent surprise?

A. There was not.

Question by Capt. H. -- Was any portion of the squadron, or any company, formed in order after passing inside of the bars, and <illegible> at the houses?

A. There was not.

Question by Capt. H. Was the command "Charge" given by Capt. Thornton preceded by any command to get the squadron in order?

A. It was not.

Question by Capt. H. Did you hear, or see, any effort to <attempt> to do so, by anyone, at that time?

A. I did not.

Question by Capt. H. In what order were the men when the charge was <called>?

A. They were in no order at all, scattered around.

Question by Capt. H. When the retreat commenced, in what direction did Capt. Thornton turn?

A. To the right.

Question by Capt. H. In what order was the squadron when the turn to the right was made?

A. In great confusion.

Question by Capt. H. Did you hear any command given after the one of which you have spoken, as from Capt. Thornton to "halt and pull down the fence" and did Capt. Thornton halt in person, after giving this command?

A. I heard no command given after this. Capt. Thornton reined up his horse, but did not halt still, that I saw.

Question by Capt. H. Did any men halt, or was any effort made to obey the command?

A. None of the men halted, but some made efforts to stop their horses. They were too much frightened and the men could not hold them in.

Question by Capt. H. When the retreat commenced, owing to the disorder of the command and known impossibility of escaping over the chaparral fence, did or did you not consider that yourself and every other man was justified in seeking his own safety by any means in his power?

A. I did.

Question by Capt. H. In what direction was Capt. Thornton going when he ran against you?

A. He was skirting the interior of the fence.

Question by Capt. H. What was the probable number of the enemy which lined the exterior part of the fence when you last saw Capt. Thornton?

A. I suppose there were some 1000 or 2000 men, principally cavalry.

Question by Capt. H. Were Capt. Thornton and the men who with him were skirting the exterior of the fence in a position which enabled them to attack or resist the enemy?

A. They could neither resist nor attack. They could have attacked them with their carbines if they could have stopped their horses.

Question by Capt. H. Was it, or not, possible for any horse in the squadron to <climb> the chaparral fence which enclosed the field into which Capt. Thornton entered with his command?

A. I think it was impossible. I have <never> seen a horse which I thought could do it.

Question by Capt. H. Did you see, after the first charge, any body of your men acting in concert, and making an organized resistance to, or attack upon, the enemy?

A. I did not.

Question by Capt. H. What was my <illegible>, <illegible>, and bearing, when I rode up to you, after you were dismounted, and asked if you were wounded?

A. You appeared to be cool and collected, and in <illegible>, not at all excited.

Question by Capt. H., Did you see the official report before I sent to it to Gen. Taylor; and if so, what opinion did you express respecting it?

A. I did see it, and approved of it, as I thought it gave a faithful account of the transaction. After making a copy of the report, furnished by the Recorder, I saw no reason for changing my opinion.

Question by Capt. H. <Were you> present when Capt. Thornton and myself <met> in Matamoros at Gen. Ampudia's, and if so, <can> you state what conversation took place between us respecting the action and any report of the same?

A. I was present, and at the conversation which ensued between Capt. Thornton and Capt. Hardee. The substance of the conversation was on the surprise and subsequent capture, and Capt. Hardee's report to Gen. Taylor about the transaction. Capt. Thornton approved of Capt. Hardee's course. He had some slight objection to the report of a want of caution, saying that we had done all we could do, and that he did not care a damn what was said provided his reputation for gallantry for preserved.

Question by Capt. H. Did I, or not, state to Capt. Thornton, at the above time and place, fully and explicitly, everything that I had written in my official report, and was this or not previous to his own report of that affair?

A. You did; and <inquired> to me to know if you had done so. I replied you had. This was previous to Capt. Thornton's report.

Question by Capt. H. Did, or not, Capt. Thornton attempt to reach the houses by the <illegible> of the field?

A. I thought he did.

Question by Capt. H. Before Capt. Thornton gave the order, to pull down the fence, did you, or not, hear me tell him that our only hope of safety was in pulling down the fence?

A. I heard you say something, but I did not understand what it was.

Question by the Court. What kind of an obstacle did the interior fence present to the passage of men or horses?

A. The fence was from 4 to 5 feet high, made of chaparral, and very difficult to leap over owing to the <dense> brush on each side.

Question by the Court. What is the distance from the place of attack to Fort Brown?

A. Between 25 and 30 miles.

Question by the Court. Will the witness state in what position, and in what condition, he saw the men of the command while he himself was crossing the cross fences referred to in the last question?

A. They were attempting to jump over the fence, and scattered about in disorder and confusion.

The signature of Capt. Bliss, Asst. Adjt. Genl., to a copy of Capt. Hardee's official report of the engagement of Capt. Thornton's command with the Mexicans on the 25th of April 1846, having sworn to by Lt. Kane, the document was received by the court, and is appended /marked B/

The court adjourned at 1 1/2 o'clock P.M. to meet again at 10 A.M. on Wednesday the 27th of May 1846.

<u>Second day</u>

Camp of the 5th Infantry
May 27th 1846

The court met pursuant to adjournment.

Present all members with recorder.

Capt. Thornton, 2d Dragoons, a witness on the part of Capt. Hardee, being duly sworn, says, On, or about, the 24th of April 1846, at the Camp Opposite Matamoros, after organizing the advanced guard, which was commanded by a sergeant, I moved with a squadron, the advanced guard proceeding it. After proceeding some 15 miles, I halted the squadron placing <two> sentries about a quarter of a mile from the squadron, each way, up and down the road, to guard against surprise.

After resting about an hour and a half, I ordered the squadron to move on. When <near> the enemy, as I supposed from information derived from some Mexicans, I strengthened the advanced guard, placing Lt. Mason in charge of it, with orders to keep one fourth of a mile ahead of the squadron, to proceed with great care, stating to him these words -- I fear an ambuscade. After proceeding a short distance I halted the squadron, it having a strong position, and dispatched Srgt. Tredo with eight men, to penetrate to the river, if possible, and reconnoiter the river with a view of discovering the enemy. He returned and stated that he had reconnoitered the river, up and down, one mile. I think I also directed him to <penetrate> by the rear of the plantation in which the squadron was when it afterwards discovered the enemy. Srgt. Tredo stated to me that he was unable to get into the plantation. I then ordered the squadron on. After proceeding a quarter of a mile I rode on to the advanced guard, halted it, and directed Lt. Mason to send the interpreter, Srgt. Lenz, and one man, to the houses in the plantation, for the purpose of getting information of the enemy. Lt. Mason said he thought the road <turned> a short distance ahead, and requested permission to proceed on a short distance from there, with a view of finding the entrance. I directed him to proceed on, and halt should he find one. After proceeding a short distance, he came to a pair of draw bars and halted. I left the squadron and rode up to the advanced guard and rode through the draw-bars, in the direction of the houses, directing the interpreter to accompany me. As I approached the houses I saw a small party of armed men running. I looked around and beckoned with my hand to the advanced guard to follow me, not knowing that the squadron had closed upon the advanced guard.

The squadron followed the advanced guard into the field, without orders from me so to do, or any intention that it should. My own attention being directed to the party above stated I continued to ride on, and when the advanced guard reached me I directed two of the men to pursue, and bring me back one of the armed Mexicans with a view of getting information of the enemy.

They did so, and when I was engaged in questioning the Mexican, the enemy was discovered by one of my squadron, making rapidly for the draw bars. I immediately ordered the squadron to charge, with a view to secure the draw bars and cut my way through back to camp, <agreeably> to my orders. The enemy got possession of the draw bars with their infantry, and held it, notwithstanding on the efforts of the squadron to force them back. The squadron swerved to the right, and galloped up the fence. I rode after them, ordered them to halt when I reached it, and directed them to break down the fence. The enemy, at this time, was firing into them, at this point. The men continued to gallop on. My horse becoming unmanageable ran with me and shortly afterward fell upon me in the field. I was unable to rise. I heard the firing going on beyond me, when suddenly it ceased. I saw nothing more of the squadron. Some half hour previous to meeting with the enemy I remarked to Lt. Kane that the guide sent with squadron, Chipeta, had caused me to suspect him by his suspicious movements, that I believed he had betrayed us, and that we should have to cut our way through the enemy back to camp. I then gave him, Lt. Kane, precise instructions what to do in such an event. I stated to him that I should endeavor to open a way for the squadron myself, directing him to keep close to me with the squadron in order to prevent the opening I should make being closed up by the enemy. About half a mile from the draw bars above mentioned I discovered a trail heading through the chaparral in the direction of the prairie. Upon examining it, I discovered that a large body of cavalry had recently passed along it in the direction of the prairie. I followed it with squadron some 2 or 3 miles, but not seeing anything of them I returned with the squadron and continued my route up the river in the direction of the crossing where I had been ordered to proceed. This body of the enemy I believe to be the one which gained my rear, as stated to me afterward by two Mexican officers. I repeatedly ordered the men to keep <profound silence>, and to keep their sabers, as far as possible, from making a noise. These orders were given by me, to prevent the enemy from discovering my approach. I directed Capt. Hardee to take his position in rear of the squadron, thinking it highly probable it might be attacked in the rear. When I gave the order to the men to halt and break down the fence I heard the order repeated by Capt. Hardee in my rear.

The appended sketch /marked A/ was shown to the witness, who pronounced it accurate.

By request of Capt. Hardee, the order convening the court, and the paper he submitted / marked C/ was read to the witness.

Question by Capt. Hardee. Have you seen Capt. Hardee's official report of the affair of April 25th?

Answer. I have not.

Question by Capt. H. It is said that there is some contradiction between this report and that made by yourself. Will you take the report made by me, of which a copy is now in possession of the court, and say if you perceive any discrepancy, and if so, in what it consists?

A copy of Capt. Thornton's report of the affair of the 25th of April was shown to the witness. He <admitted> its correctness when it was received by the court /appended marked D./

Answer. I perceive no discrepancies between the reports, my report being a short and very general one.

Question by Capt. H. Will you state in what particulars you consider the report made by me as inaccurate, if at all?

A. If by that part of the report, vis "to these houses Capt. Thornton endeavored, by entering the lower extremity, to approach," a party detached from my command, and not myself individually, is understood, the sentence is not inaccurate. Capt. Hardee is mistaken in that portion of his report, "Capt. Thornton was prepossessed with the idea that the Mexicans had not crossed, and if they had they would not fight." That portion of the report which states, "When I came up to the houses, I found the men scattered in every direction," is a <decided> inaccuracy. "Seeing this Capt. Thornton turned to the right and skirted the interior of the fence, the command following him," is inaccurate. The squadron, or a portion of it, had turned to the right, and were going up the fence, when I turned my horse and followed after it.

Question by Capt. H. Did, or did not, witnesses state to him on the road, more than once, that he would believe that the enemy had crossed when he saw them?

A. I may have made the remark prior to the information given me by the Mexicans that the enemy had crossed about three miles from the place where we discovered the enemy, though I am not positive.

Question by Capt. Hardee. Did <not the> witness state to me, more than once, that to fight the Mexicans he wanted his company to be armed with whips alone?

A. I have frequently made use of the remark in camp, though I do not remember having made it on this occasion.

Question by Capt. H. On the arrival of the witness in Matamoros, did I state to him what course I had pursued in the whole affair, and if so, what opinion did the witness express respecting that course?

A. You did. I do not remember stating to Capt. Hardee my opinion of his course, further than that he had done well in surrendering the squadron. That is, that he had pursued a correct course as I believed the retreat was cut off.

The court adjourned at 2 o'clock P.M. to meet again at 10 o'clock A.M. on Thursday the 28th of May 1846.

Third day

Camp of the 5th Infantry
Thursday, May 28, 1846

The Court met pursuant to the adjournment.

Present, all the members and the recorder.

Srgt. Freeman, a witness on the part of Capt. Hardee, being duly sworn, says I was 2d sergeant of Company "F" 2d Dragoons, commanded by Capt. Thornton. On the 25th of April 1846, about 8 o'clock in the morning, being on the advanced guard, <under> charge of Lt. Mason, I had <marched> up to a field on the left side of the road. The advanced guard halted at an opening where bars were placed. Capt. Thornton rode forward, and ordered the bars to be let down. There were some Mexicans in the field, near the houses. They were mounted. After the bars were let down, Capt. Thornton rode into the field at a gallop, and halted half way from the bars to the houses. The Mexicans at the houses were making their retreat at that time. Capt. Thornton then made a signal to advance. I, being on the right of the advanced guard, galloped in the field. On arriving abreast of Capt. Thornton, I was commanded to halt. After I had halted, Capt. Thornton advanced up on a hill, followed by the advanced guard and by the squadron. Capt. Thornton ordered me to go and take one man and bring him back a prisoner, and not <shoot> him. I brought the Mexican to Capt. Thornton. The men, at that time on the hill, were mostly dismounted, some getting water in the bayou, and some lying on the ground holding their horses. Capt. Thornton then inquired about the Mexicans and the crossings, but before he could get any satisfactory reply from him, there was an alarm given from the direction of the bars. Capt. Thornton called out "there are the Mexicans--thousands of them. Mount men, draw your sabers, and charge," the captain heading on in advance about fifty yards. I should judge about 15 men followed Capt. Thornton. In making the charge Capt. Thornton made a semi-circle in approaching the bars. The rest of the men, who could get their horses, mounted them, and followed on after Capt. Thornton. After making the charge some three or four men, who had mounted after Capt. Thornton had off, called out that the order was, "Every man for himself." This was immediately after the charge was had off, but who the man was I cannot say. I turned my horse to the right.

These men were making their retreat toward a cross fence and were on my right and a little to my rear. I called to them and could get no reply from them. I then made my own retreat as there was no one in the field at the time but myself, that I could see. After I had arrived at the cross fence, in my retreat, there were some men jumping the fence. Lt. Kane had crossed at that time. I then turned to the left, in an oblique direction, and in crossing the cane brake, my horse <mired> down, and I was taken prisoner.

The sketch /marked A/ was shown to the witness, who said that it was a correct one.

Question by Capt. Hardee. How far was the advanced guard ahead of the squadron when you entered the field?

A. About 200 yards, as near as I could judge. I did not look behind.

Question by Capt. H. In what order was the squadron formed when halting at the houses, and at the moment when Capt. Thornton gave the command "charge"?

A. In the greatest disorder.

Question by Capt. H. From the time the retreat commenced, what <were> you endeavoring to do yourself and what did you think others were doing?

A. I was endeavoring to save myself and I thought others were doing the same.

Question by Capt. H. Did you, at any time after the retreat commenced, see any number of your men acting in concert together? Did you hear any orders given nor see any attack made upon or resistance to the enemy?

A. I did not after I heard the remark made by the men, "Every man for himself." They were in retreat at that time.

Capt. Hardee <then> read a paper to the court of which the following is a copy.

I will state to the court that my object in getting a narration from these witnesses is to bring before the minds of the Court as clear and lively a realization as is possible of the exact character of this short affair, and also to put them before the court in the widest and fullest sense, to be examined on any, <or any> points upon which, in the opinion of the court, any light is "<needed>".

Question by the Court. Was any portion of the enemy's force within the enclosure, in the neighborhood of the bars, before the retreat commenced? If so, how were they drawn up?

A. There was a body of about 100 infantry inside of the bars, in the field, formed in line along the road heading from the bars to the houses, with their right flank in the direction of Capt. Thornton's squadron before charging. A body of lancers were outside of the bars, across the road, drawn up in line fronting the infantry.

Question by the Court. What number of the enemy did you suppose to be in, and around the field, when the retreat commenced?

A. I was under the impression that there were two or three thousand.

Private William McConnell, of Company C. 2d Dragoons, a witness on the part of Capt. Hardee, being duly sworn, says, I was one of Capt. Thornton's command on the 25th of April. I was about two-thirds of the way to the rear in the squadron, when we approached the bars. Capt. Thornton entered the bars first himself, and went up toward the houses at a gallop, called for Srgt. Freeman to follow him, and then <motioned> to the remainder of the squadron to come in, which they did by jumping the bars in single file. They all galloped up to the houses, and scattered around, some looking in at the doors, others at the windows, some dismounted going to get water at the pond, some to light their pipes, some lying on the pommel of their saddles. A man on my right said "the Mexicans are coming in at the bars," and repeated it to Capt. Thornton. I suppose he did not hear him. Srgt. Tredo told him afterwards. Capt. Thornton rode in front of the command and said, "Jesus Christ there's thousands of them--draw your sabers men, and charge." All this time he was advancing toward the enemy. When Capt. Thornton came in front of the men, and before he gave the command "charge" Capt. Hardee said, "form men, form men," repeatedly, "as well as you can." Then Capt. Thornton bolted off at full speed, and I followed him. I got a little ahead of Capt. Thornton, to his right, and while getting ready to fire my carbine, Capt. Thornton wheeled to his right, and I did not see any more of him. Then I galloped toward the road fence on my right. The fence was too high to leap, so I galloped toward the retreating party, in an oblique direction to the right.

I saw Lt. Kane and horse fall at this time, at a bush cross fence, <near me>. I galloped toward another part of the field where I saw a party of our men collected together, trying to cross over. I passed this party and rode across the field where I saw some men retreating under command of Capt. Hardee. I followed Capt. Hardee over a precipice and through a cane brake to a field on the opposite side, where we fell in with some more of our men. Capt. Hardee ordered us to fall into our platoons, and to be ready to fight. He asked if there was any possibility of our crossing the river. One of the men, I believe the orderly sergeant, said that he had tried it, but that the horses would <mire> before they could get to it. Then he ordered the men again to form, and be ready to fight as quickly as possible. Some said they had lost their carbines, others their sabers, and others their pistols, and complained that they had nothing to fight with. The orderly Srgt. told Capt Hardee that the men thought there was a good deal of danger, and that they would be surrendered and showed a disposition not to fight. Capt. Hardee asked the Orderly Srgt. who did not wish to fight? And if he did not, <repeatedly>.

He replied, yes he would fight. The men again said they thought it was best not to fight, when Capt. Hardee asked for a white handkerchief, and passed the remark that he did not suppose they would <show> us any quarter, but he would try, which he did. To hold ourselves in readiness, and if they did not we would sell our lives as dear as possible. When the white flag went out, Capt. Hardee ordered us to be ready if they would not receive it.

They received the flag and called Capt. Hardee. We were then taken prisoners.

Question by Capt. Hardee. Did you, at any time after the retreat commenced, see any <number> of your men acting in concert together. Did you hear any orders given, or see any attack made upon, or resistance to, the enemy?

Answer. I did not, until I came up with Capt. Hardee.

Question by Capt. Hardee. From the time the retreat commenced, what were you endeavoring to do yourself, and what did you think others were doing?

A. I think every man was trying to save himself, as well as he could. I was.

Question by Capt. Hardee. What numbers of the enemy did you suppose to be in, and around, the field, when the retreat commenced?

A. I think between two and three thousand.

Srgt. Clark, of Compy. C 2d Dragoons, a witness for Capt. Hardee, being duly sworn, says

On the 25th of April my position in the squadron under Capt. Thornton was in the rear of all except Capt. Hardee, the squadron marching in single file when passing the bars. We were twenty odd miles above our camp and <illegible> the river. Upon arriving at the houses the squadron was in a perfect state of disorder, scattered to the right and left, part of the men mounted and some dismounted, some getting water having obtained permission of Capt. Thornton in my hearing. A few moments after this I heard the command "charge" from Capt. Thornton, and mounted my horse as soon as possible, and on arriving at the summit of the hill, in sight of Capt. Thornton, saw him brandish his saber over his head, immediately after which the word was passed "Every man on his own hook." A few moments previous to this, and, I think, after the command "charge", I heard Capt. Hardee urging the men to get into some kind of order. The next I saw of Capt. Hardee was at the river, into which I had jumped my horse, and finding it impossible to get through, as it was so <miry>, returned to the bank, and heard Capt. Hardee enquiring whether we could not pass the river. I replied that it was impossible as I had just attempted it and liked to have mired my horse. Capt. Hardee ordered the little command, which had collected around, to follow him. We went up from the river a short distance and halted and Capt. Hardee ordered me to form the men and enquired the numbers. I reported twenty-five present. Capt. Hardee said it would be necessary to make a desperate effort, as we probably would be shown no quarter. Several of the men, at the same time, said it would be best to surrender, as we were entirely surrounded and many of us had lost our arms. Capt. Hardee told us we should be prepared in case they did not respect the flag which was about to be put out. He appeared to doubt whether they would. The flag was sent, and Capt. Hardee stated to the Mexican officer who was sent forward, that he would surrender us prisoners of war and on no other conditions. I heard this distinctly. We were accepted as prisoners of war.

Question by Capt. Hardee. Did you, or not, hear Capt. Hardee call upon the men, at any time, to follow him, and if so, when was it?

Answer. Yes, when we came up from the river.

Question by Capt. H. Did you see, at the time the charge was attempted, any of the enemy inside of the bars? If so, how were they placed, and were they cavalry, infantry, or both?

A. At the time Capt. Thornton wheeled to the right I saw the enemy inside the bars. They appeared to be infantry.

The court adjourned at 2 o'clock to be in <court> again at 10 o'clock A.M. on Friday the 29th of May 1846.

<u>Fourth day</u>

Camp of the 5th Infantry
Friday, May 29th, 1846

The Court met pursuant to adjournment.
Present, all the members and the recorder.

Private Frederick Lavoisien of Compy. C 2d Dragoons, a witness on the part of Capt.
Hardee, having been duly sworn, says

On the morning of the 25th of April last I was towards the rear of Capt. Thornton's
squadron. The squadron passed through the bars in single file. They went toward some
houses near the river, and when I arrived there, they were pressing around Capt. Thornton
to see a Mexican taken by Srgt. Freeman, and brought before Capt. Thornton. Some were
dismounted, getting water, others holding their horses. Capt. Thornton told the men to
keep back. The men scattered and moved back, I with them. I rode up among the houses.
I turned my horse a short time after, two or three minutes, and saw the Mexicans coming
through the chaparral on the other side of the fence. I first told Private McConnell, of
C Compy., there the Mexicans are, and then reported it to Srgt. Tredo, who reported it
to Capt. Thornton. Capt. Thornton immediately wheeled his horse around, and drew his
saber. The only command I heard him give was "charge." I heard Capt. Hardee say immediately afterwards, "form, as well as you can, men," or words to that effect. I drew my saber
and rode off, right after McConnell and Srgt. Tredo, towards the gap. Capt. Thornton was
about 20 yards ahead of us. Capt. Thornton fired his pistol among the enemy, and by that
time McConnell and myself had arrived within 10 yards of him. I saw him wave his saber,
and wheel his horse to the right. I followed in that direction. In a <corner>, near the first
cross fence, I saw Capt. Thornton again. I heard no order at all. Every man, at that time,
seemed to be looking out for himself. I rode down the fence about 100 yards and jumped
over it into another field. I passed several men on the way. No two men were going the
same way, and they did not seem to be acting in concert at all. In crossing another fence
I saw Capt. Thornton's horse standing by the edge of the chaparral, without a rider. I rode
on then and turned down the river. I saw several men riding in the same direction. Some
proposed to go in one way, some in another. We had no one to lead us. In a few minutes
Capt. Hardee rode up followed by McConnell. There might have been others following
them, but I did not see them, or if I did, I did not know them. Capt. Hardee asked if there
was no way of escape; whether we could cross the river, or not. Some of the men answered
that we could not. Capt. Hardee asked if they had tried. Some one, or more, said they
had, and that they found it too boggy for their horses to get across. Capt. Hardee then
said that these people would not show us any quarter, in all probability, and proposed to
make a desperate charge, and sell our lives as dearly as possible. He told the Srgt. to form
the men and find out how many there were. The Srgt. told him there were 25 men. Capt.
Hardee then asked who was for fighting? Some said "this is no use, we are surrounded,"
and others, among them was myself, said we had lost our arms, or most of them.

Capt. Hardee then went around and inspected the arms. Almost everyone had lost some-
thing. I had lost my carbine and saber. Someone proposed showing a white flag. Capt.
Hardee sent me out with the flag. He then rode forward and met a Mexican officer, and
I understood him to say to him, that on condition of our being treated as prisoners of

war, we would surrender. We dismounted, and they made us lead our horses to where the commanding officer was.

Private James Orr, of Compy. F 2d Dragoons, a witness on the part of Capt. Hardee, being duly sworn, was asked by Capt. Hardee,

On the 25th of April last, after the fight of Capt. Thornton's command with the Mexicans was over, did you, or did you not, attempt crossing the river with your horse?

A. I did. At the edge of the water it was muddy and boggy, and it was impossible for any horse to cross.

Question by Capt. H. After being mired, did you bring your horse out of your own accord, or were you ordered to do so?

A. I came out of my own accord. I heard some of the men say that Capt. Hardee had ordered me out, but I did not hear him. Capt. Hardee was on the bank of the river.

Capt. Hardee then submitted a paper, of which the following is a copy.

"I have now placed before the court the evidence of the only two surviving officers of the captured squadron, beside myself, one of these its commanding officer. Of a sergeant and private from Capt. Thornton's compy, of a sergeant and two privates from my own, these latter being selected according to the best of my judgment as those likely to know most of the whole transaction. No doubt, however, many others may be found equally capable of giving testimony, and in view of the position in which I am placed, and with accomplishment of the objects stated by me in the commencement of my case, I have now to request of the court, as a favor to myself, that they call before them any other witnesses whom they may select from the squadron, and subject them to examination for themselves, <respecting> on the points embraced in the paper read by me to the court, or any other points of the transaction in question."

Capt. Larnard, 4th Infantry, a witness on the part of Capt. Hardee, being duly sworn, says,

I think on the evening of the second day after Capt. Hardee's official report arrived in our camp, I was standing amid a group composed of several officers of the 4th Infantry and other regiments. The conversation was on the subject of Capt. Thornton's capture. An officer there stated that some officers of Capt. Hardee's Rgt. said that it was evident that he, Capt. Hardee, had deserted his commanding officer and carried off 25 men with him. I afterward heard from other officers expressions of opinion more or less unfavorable to Capt. Hardee, with reference to his conduct in this transaction, and also expressions from some officers to the effect that there was direct contradictions between the official report presented by Capt. Hardee and that presented by Capt. Thornton.

Col. D. E. Twiggs, 2d Dragoons, a witness on the part of Capt. Hardee, being duly sworn, was asked by Capt. Hardee,

Have you heard any imputations against the conduct of Capt. Hardee in the affair of the 25th of April, and if so, of what nature were those imputations?

A. I have heard imputations from one or more persons. It was in this, that when Capt. Thornton ordered a charge, Capt. Hardee gave different orders, and for this he was censorable, as they said the commanding officer was responsible, and his orders should not be interfered with in an important and <delicate> affair like this. I have heard many remark that there was a positive contradiction between the two reports of Capts. Thornton and Hardee, one saying that there was an advanced guard, and the other saying that there was not.

Question by Capt. H. Did you, or not, hear Capt. Hardee charged with having deserted his commanding officer and carried off 25 men with him?

A. I am not certain, but I don't think I have. I, myself, have made no imputations against Capt. Hardee.

Capt. C. A. May, 2d Dragoons, a witness on the part of Capt. Hardee, being duly sworn, was asked by Capt. Hardee,

Have you heard any imputations against the conduct of Capt. Hardee in the affair of the 25th of April, and, if so, of what nature were the imputations?

A. I have heard, as every officer in the Army must have heard, different opinions expressed upon the subject of the capture of Capt. Thornton's command. Some of these opinions reflected upon Capt. Hardee, others defended him. It was a subject of common camp talk, and if a difference of opinion had not existed I presume it would not have been discussed.

Question by Capt. H. Have you heard it asserted that there were important contradictions between the official reports of Capts. Thornton and Hardee?

A. I have.

Question by Capt. H. Have you heard it said that Capt. Hardee deserted his commanding officer, and carried off 25 men with him?

A. I have heard the opinion expressed, in the course of conversation on this subject, which inference was drawn from Capt. Hardee's report, that in consequence of finding that Capt. Thornton was leading his men to destruction that he ordered a portion to follow him, this without the authority of Capt. Thornton, or without consulting him. That he did leave him with a party of men, <illegible> being twenty five.

That I have heard it very harshly spoken of, and that I myself believed and spoke of it, that Capt. Hardee had assumed a responsibility that his commission did not entitle him to. The opinions that I heard expressed, and that I expressed myself, was formed from his own report.

At the request of Capt. Hardee, in order to afford him time to prepare his final statement, the court adjourned at 1 o'clock P. M. to meet again at 12 A. M. on Saturday the 30th of May 1846.

Fifth day

Camp of the 5th Infantry
Saturday, May 30th, 1846

The court met pursuant to adjournment.

Present all members and the recorder.

As Capt. Hardee was not prepared, the court, at his request, immediately adjourned to meet again at 9 A. M. on Sunday, the 31st of May 1846.

Sixth day

Camp of the 5th Infantry
Sunday, May 31, 1846

The court met pursuant to adjournment.

Present, all the members and the recorder.

Capt. Hardee submitted the paper appended and marked E.

The proceedings were read to the Court.

The Court directed the recorder to procure from the Hd. Quarters of the 2d Rgt. of Dragoons a list of the men surrendered by Capt. Hardee on the 25th of April last, and to select from this, at random, and summon, on the part of the court, <six> men as witnesses, taking a <like number> from each of the two companies engaged.

The court adjourned at 1 o'clock P. M. to meet again on Thursday, the 4th of May 1846, at 10 o'clock A. M. the interval required to obtain the witnesses from Point Isabel.

<u>Seventh day</u>

Camp of the 5th Infantry
Thursday, June 4th, 1846

The court met pursuant to adjournment.

Present all the members and the recorder.

Srgt. Lenz, a witness on the part of the Court, being duly sworn, was asked by the Court the following questions.

What was your Company and Regt. on the 25th of April last?

A. F. Company, 2d Dragoons, commanded by Capt. S. B. Thornton.

Q. Were you with Capt. Thornton's command in the affair of the 25th of April last? If so, what was your position in the squadron at the time of entering the bars?

A. I was. I was ahead of the squadron and followed Capt. Thornton into the field when he beckoned.

Q. With what front, and in what order, did the squadron pass the bars into the enclosure?

A. I don't know. The men rushed in, and Capt. Thornton reprimanded Srgt. Freeman particularly for it.

Q. After the squadron entered the enclosure, in what order was it? Describe what part of it, if any, was in order of battle?

A. In no order. No portion of the squadron was in order of battle. Some were listening to the Mexicans, some were dismounted getting water, some looking in at the houses.

Q. When the command charge was given, in what order was the squadron?

A. In the same disorder as just put down.

Q. After Capt. Thornton gave the command to charge, did you hear Capt. Hardee give any commands; if so what were they?

A. I did not hear any.

Q. Did you hear any order to the squadron to close up with the advance guard on arriving at the bars, and before entering the plantation?

A. I did not.

Q. What was Capt. Hardee's behavior throughout the affair, as far as it came to your observation, with reference to courage and soldierly conduct, good or otherwise, describe it.

A. By trying to collect the men in going to the river and in surrendering I thought he saved our lives. He was cool and his conduct was good. He wanted us to fight.

The court instructed the recorder to put the same questions to the witnesses examined subsequently by the court. The questions are referred to by the figures in the record.

Francis O'Neill, as witness on the part of the court, was duly sworn.

1st Question, Answer. F Compy, 2d Dragoons.

2d Question. Answer. I was, and was in the rear of the squadron.

3d Question. Answer. Some passed in single file, and some in double. I did not think they went in orderly. Some were walking, some running, some jumped over the bars before they were let down.

4th Question. Answer. I was getting water and could not see. There were three or four men with me.

The witness knew nothing in relation to the 5th, 6th, and 7th questions.

8th Question. Answer. I thought Capt. Hardee behaved like a courageous man and if we had followed his advice we would have been better off.

Private Brown, a witness on the part of the court, was duly sworn.

1st Question. Answer. F Compy. 2d Dragoons.

2nd Question. Answer. I was. I was about the middle of the squadron.

3d. Question. Answer. They went in by single file, in an orderly way.

4th. Question. Answer. They were in no order at all. They were riding about looking in at the houses. Some were dismounted getting water. I saw no portion in line of battle.

5th Question. Answer. In the order I have mentioned.

6th Question. Answer. I did not hear him. I charged with Capt. Thornton.

7th Question. Answer. I did not.

8th Question. Answer. When I saw him he was forming the men who had retreated. He was cool and collected and behaved like a brave man, and like an officer.

Private Fitzgerald, a witness on the part of the Court, being duly sworn.

1st Question. Answer. "F" Compy 2d Dragoons.

2d Question. Answer. I was, and in the advanced guard.

3d Question. Answer. I was ahead and could not see.

4th Question. Answer. Scattered around, some looking at the houses, some were dismounted, getting water. More than half were mounted. I was engaged in searching the houses. I did not see any order of battle, and were in the way I have described, scattered about.

5th Question. Answer. The same order.

6th Question. Answer. I do not recollect Capt. Hardee giving any order.

7th Question. Answer. <No sir.>

8th Question. Answer. No man could have acted better. He formed his men to make a last and desperate charge, as a soldier ought to do. I was with him at the time.

Private Allen, a witness on the part of the Court was duly sworn.

1st Question. Answer. Capt. Hardee's Company "C" 2d Dragoons.

2nd Question. Answer. I was, and about the center of the squadron.

3d Question. Answer. In single file. They walked up to the bars and went into a slow gallop after getting over them.

4th Question. Answer. In no order. Some were mounted, and about a dozen dismounted, I think. There might have been more. We were in no order of battle.

5th Question. Answer. There was no order about it.

6th and 7th Questions. Answers. I did not hear any.

8th Question. Answer. He acted as a soldier should. I saw him when the men were collecting at the river.

Corpl. Frasier, a witness on the part of the court, was duly sworn.

1st Question. Answer. Compy. C 2d Dragoons.

2d Question. Answer. I was. I was the last man who entered the bars.

3d Question. Answer. <One line> and then went over together. No order was given to form <illegible>. We had been marching in single file.

4th Question. Answer. About one third of the men were dismounted and there was confusion.

5th Question. Answer. The same order.

6th Question. Answer. I heard him give the command "draw your sabers and form as well as you can men." No order had been given to draw sabers before.

7th Question. Answer. I did not. I was in rear.

8th Question. Answer. He behaved with the greatest coolness and bravery.

When the last question was put to each witness, and before being answered, Capt. Hardee, at his own request, was permitted to withdraw.

After maturely weighing the testimony presented, the Court finds the following.

<u>Facts</u>

On the 24th of April 1846 a squadron of the 2d Regt. of Dragoons consisting of companies "F" and "C" /Thornton and Hardee/ commanded by Capt. Thornton, left the Encampment of the Army of Occupation on the Rio Bravo, opposite Matamoros, proceeding up and contiguous to the river, to ascertain what force of the enemy, if any, had crossed the river, and the position of that force. The next morning, the 25th, between 8 and 10 o'clock, and between 25 and 30 miles from the encampment of the Army, the squadron entered a large field, or plantation, bordering on the river, in which there were some Mexican houses, the entrance to the same being by draw bars, the plantations being divided into several fields by chaparral fences and brush, and the whole being enclosed with a high post or chaparral fence, impracticable for a horse.

The advanced guard of the squadron, consisting of one subaltern and ten men, halted at the bars, the squadron having closed up with it without authority from Capt. Thornton for as it appears from the testimony. Capt. Thornton entered the enclosure, advanced about 100 yards in the direction of the houses, and beckoned for the squadron, or a por-tion of it, to advance, and ordered the leading men to <illegible> one of some Mexicans who were running from the houses, which were about 100 yards from him. The squadron then entered the bars in single file in some disorder at different rates of speed, running, galloping, trotting, and no guard was placed in advance of the plantation, and no sentinel left at the bars. After entering the plantation, and on nearing the houses, no part of the squadron was in order of battle, the men being scattered about, some getting water, some examining the houses, others reclining against their horses, a portion being dismounted. In a few minutes the enemy was discovered in front, in the direction of the bars, when Capt. Thornton gave the command "Mount, men, draw your saber, and charge." Capt. Thornton charged immediately, followed by a portion of his men. On <nearing> the bars the fire of the enemy caused the horses to swerve to the right, <rendered> them unman-ageable, and they <rode> off with their riders, the men being followed by Capt. Thornton. From that moment each was seeking his own safety, the word having been passed to that effect, originating with whom does not appear. When Capt. Thornton gave the command "charge" Capt. Hardee directed the men to form as well as they could, and charged with the squadron <and> he afterwards repeated Capt. Thornton's order to his men to halt and pull down the fence, which order was not obeyed, the men being unable to control their horses. After this Capt. Hardee collected a few of the men, led them towards the river, where he found others, until he found his party, with stragglers that afterwards joined him, amounted to 25, the greater part having lost some of their arms, either carbine, saber, or pistol. Capt. Hardee then endeavored to make his escape by the river, but finding that impracticable from the boggy nature of the soil on its margin, he proposed to the men to charge and to sell their lives as dearly as possible. Finding from the remarks of the men, and his own inspection, their unarmed condition, he concluded to surrender on the usual terms, if such terms were not guaranteed, to sell their lives as cheaply as possible. The terms were granted, the surrender was made. The strength of the enemy appeared to be about 2000 men, consisting of cavalry and infantry, principally of the former. A part of this infantry was in the field in the direction from the bars to the houses fronting the dragoons. The bars were guarded by infantry and cavalry, and the cavalry surrounded the plantation.

The Court is therefore of

Opinion

1st. That the conduct of Capt. W. J. Hardee, of the 2d Regt. of Dragoons, in the affair of the 25th of April 1846 between Capt. Thornton's command and the Mexican forces, was, in all respects, that of an intelligent and gallant soldier, that he did all in his power, by word and deed, to sustain his commanding officer in the discharge of his duty, and that any imputation against his character, growing out of his conduct as connected with that affair, is utterly without foundation.

2d. That the official report of Capt. Hardee to the Commanding General of the Army of Occupation, dated Matamoros, Mexico, April 26th 1846, is correct in all its particulars.

The court adjourned at 2 o'clock P. M. to meet again on Friday the 5th of June 1846 at 12 AM.

Eighth day

Camp of the 5th Infantry
Friday June 5th, 1846

The court met pursuant to adjournment.

President, all its members and the recorder.

The proceedings since the 5th day of the session were read to the court.

The court, having no further business, adjourned sine die.

<W. H. Churchill signature> Recorder

<T. Staniford signature> President of the Court

Hd. Qu. Army of Occupation
Matamoros, June 8, 1846

The proceedings and opinion of the court are approved
Z. Taylor
Bvt. Brig. Gen'l, Commdg.

/A/

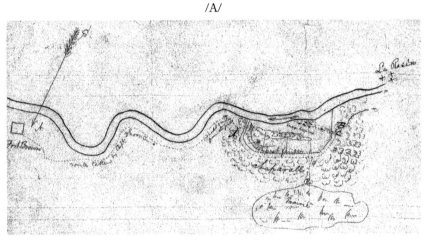

Credit: National Archives

/B/

Matamoros, Mexico
April 26, 1846

It becomes my painful duty to inform you of the circumstances which led to our being brought to this place as prisoners of war. Capt. Thornton's command consisting of fifty-two dragoons left camp, as you know, at night on the 24th instant; it marched 15 miles and halted until daylight when the march was again resumed. Capt. Thornton's orders, as I understood them, were to ascertain if the enemy had crossed the river above our camp and to reconnoiter his position in force. All his inquiries on the way tended to the conviction that the enemy had crossed in strength. About 28 miles from our camp our guide became so satisfied of the fact that he refused to go any further and no entreaties on the part of Capt. Thornton could shake his resolution. About three miles from the latter place we came to a large plantation bordering on the river and enclosed with a high chaparral fence with some houses at the upper extremity. To these houses Capt. Thornton endeavored, by entering the lower extremity, to approach, but failing to do so was compelled to pass around the fence, and entered the field by a pair of bars, the house is being situated about 200 yards from the entrance. Into this plantation the whole command entered in single file, without any guard being placed in front, without any sentinel at the bars, or any other precautions being taken to prevent surprise. Capt. Thornton was prepossessed with the idea that the Mexicans had not crossed, and if they had that they would not fight. I had been placed in rear and was therefore the last to enter, when I came up to the houses I found the men scattered in every direction, hunting for someone with whom to communicate. At last an old man was found, and while Capt. Thornton was talking to him the cry of alarm was given and the enemy was seen in numbers at the bars. Our gallant commander immediately gave the command to charge and himself led the advance, but it was too late, the enemy had secured the entrance and it was impossible to force it. The officers and men did everything that fearless intrepidity could accomplish, but the infantry had stationed themselves in the field on the right of the passageway and the cavalry lined the exterior fence and our retreat was hopelessly cut off. Seeing this Capt. Thornton turned to the right and skirted the interior of the fence, the command following him. During this time the enemy were shooting at us in every direction and when the retreat commenced our men were in a perfect state of disorder. I rode up to Captain Thornton and told him that our only hope of safety was in tearing down the fence, he gave the order, but could not stop his horse nor would the men stop. It was useless, for by this time the enemy had gained our rear in great numbers. Foreseeing that the direction which Captain Thornton was pursuing would lead to the certain destruction of himself and men without the possibility of resistance, I turned to the right and told them to follow me. I made for the river intending either to swim it or place myself in a position of defense. I found the bank too boggy to accomplish the former, and therefore rallied the men, forming them into order of battle in the open field and without the range of the infantry behind a fence. I counted 25 men and examined their arms, but almost everyone had lost a saber, a pistol, or carbine, nonetheless the men were firm and disposed if necessary, to fight to the last extremity. In five minutes from the time the first shot was fired the field was surrounded by a numerous body of man, however I determined to sell our lives as dearly as possible if I could not secure good treatment. Accordingly I went forward and arranged with an officer that I should deliver myself and men as prisoners of war and be treated with all the consideration to which such unfortunates are entitled by the rules of civilized warfare. I was taken to a Gen'l Torahon, who by this time had his full force collected in the field. I found that some prisoners had already been taken, which together with those I had, and those which were subsequently brought in amounted to 45 men exclusive of Lieut. Kane and myself. Four were wounded. I know nothing certain of the fate of Capt. Thornton and Lieut. Mason; the latter I did not see after the fight commenced. I am convinced they both died bravely, the former I know was unhorsed, and killed as I learned, in single combat by Roman Falcon. Lieut. Mason's spurs were seen after the fight in possession of the enemy. The brave Sergeant Tredo fell in the first charge. Sergeant Smith was unhorsed and killed. The bodies of seven men were found including as I believe, the two officers above mentioned.

I was brought to Matamoros today about 4 o'clock, and I take pleasure in stating that since our surrender I and my brave companions in misfortune have been treated with uniform kindness and attention. It may soften the rigors of war for you to be informed fully of this fact. Lieut. Kane and myself are living with Gen'l Ampudia: we lodge in his hotel, eat at his table, and his frank, agreeable manner and generous hospitality almost make us forget our captivity. Gen'l Arista received us in the most gracious manner, said that his nation has been regarded as barbarous and that he wished to prove to us the contrary. Told Lieut. Kane and myself that we should receive half pay and our men should receive ample rations, and in lieu of it for today, 25 cents apiece. On declining the boon on the part of the Lieut. Kane and myself and a request that we might be permitted to send to camp for money, he said, No, that he could not permit it, that he intended to supply all our wants himself. These promises have already been fulfilled in full.

I am sir,
Very respectfully
W. J. Hardee
Capt. 2d Dragoons

a true copy
W.W. Bliss
ajt.

/C/

Gentlemen,

My motive in asking for the investigation which is now about to be instituted into my conduct during the affair of April 25 is twofold, first from the character and unfortunate issue of the affair itself, which renders it proper for all concerned that the circumstances should be well understood and clearly established, and because from the fact that imputations of an infamous nature have by some individuals at least been made with more or less publicity against me, and facts of my official report have been said to contradict that of Capt. Thornton my comd'g officer. My object under to the influence of these motives is, to place before you in a connected form all the facts of the transaction so far as they can be substantiated by the evidence of the actions and let the facts speak for themselves in <illegible> of my own conduct and in proof that the official report made by me is in all particulars exactly accurate. I earnestly desire to avoid as far as possible all individual reference and yet more earnestly disclaim any intention of imputing blame or censure unless in so far as may necessarily follow from the facts proven.

I have been attacked in my absence – have been <illegible> in terms the most bitter and calumnious, but in myself it is not my desire to become an assassin in turn.

With permission of the court, I will now call in evidence to prove 1st The accuracy of my official report. 2nd The character of the ground on which the surprise of April 25 took place. 3rd The exact disposition of the men at the time of the attack and their condition when the retreat commenced. 4th The state of affairs at the instant when "I called upon the men to follow me." 5th My own conduct and bearing from first to last in the transaction.

Respectfully submitted
WJ Hardee
Capt. 2d Dragoons

/D/

Matamoros, Mexico
April 27, 1846

Sir,

I have the honor to report my arrival at this place today, and I state that agreeable with your orders I preceded to within three miles of La Rusia, when I was informed that the enemy had crossed in large numbers, upon receiving the information our guide refused to go any farther. I was therefore compelled to move on without him, in order to carry out your instructions to me. The advanced guard was increased and Lieut. Mason placed in command of it, with orders to keep about one quarter of a mile ahead, when we had gone about <two> miles, I discovered some Mexicans near a house in a large field, I halted the advance guard and went into the field myself to see them. I had not gone more than a hundred yards when they fled, I turned around and motioned to the advanced guard to come on, in the meantime the main body of the squadron had come up to the advance guard and mistaking my order, followed in after them, and while I was questioning a Mexican the enemy appeared. I immediately ordered a charge in order to cut my way through them, but finding their numbers too large to contend with any longer I ordered a retreat and although entirely surrounded we endeavored to cut our way through to camp. In the retreat my horse fell upon me and I was unable to rise. I'm now fully convinced that we were watched from the time we left camp and that preparations were so made as to prevent our ever returning. It affords me great pleasure to say that the officers and men under my command both individually and collectively behaved in the most gallant manner. As a prisoner of war I am happy to inform you that attentions and kindness have been lavished upon me, and as an example of which I will state that upon my reporting to General Arista that a dragoon had treated me rudely, he ordered him immediately punished.

I have the honor to be
Sir,
Your obedient servant,
{signed} S.B. Thornton
Capt 2d Dragoons

Capt. W.W.J. Bliss
Asst. Adj. Gen'l.

a true copy

/E/

If Gentlemen in the amount of evidence it has been necessary for me to bring before you <I> have drawn at somewhat tedious length upon your attention, I shall at least be able to dispense with <making> a very short summary of this testimony and detain you with only a few short remarks which <at some points> seem to be required. The first point which as I have already stated it is my object to establish is the accuracy in all particulars of my official report. The evidence of Lieut. Kane is direct and positive upon every statement in that report (same one which <illegible illegible illegible> held by Capt. T) up to the time when the retreat was in full <progress> as entirely confirming each of these statements. Lieut. Kane also testified that he read my report before it was sent to Gen'l Taylor and when <illegible> from the short time which had elapsed since the <illegible illegible> all the incident must have been fresh in his memory; that he then considered and <illegible> it entirely accurate and still so considers it. Thornton the com'd officer of the squadron <my second> witness, declares that there is no discrepancy or contradiction between my report and his own—to his declaration I beg to call your particular attention as I shall be compelled to refer to it in another place. <illegible> stating, what is very evident, that my own report is full and detailed while his <is> brief and very <general>. Capt. T, in compliance with a request from myself, points out what he considers inaccuracies in <my> report and finds the following: 1st that I was mistaken in asserting that "Capt. T was prepossessed of the idea that the Mexicans had not crossed and <would> not fight if they had" as this was but an opinion of my own, it ought perhaps to have been expressed less positively: that my opinion was a mistaken one does not affect or impair the correctness of my report for it was certainly at that time honestly <entertained> by me and upon <illegible> <some> of which are <perhaps> sufficiently evident in the testimony which has been given. The second <disputed> accuracy is one of greatly more importance, involving the correctness

157

of a direct and positive statement made by me upon my own observation in these words: "When I came up to the houses I found the men scattered in every direction." This, says Capt. T., "is a decided inaccuracy." If so certainly a most important one both in itself and in its <bearings>. Lieut. Kane in answer to a question on this point says that no portion of the squadron or of the company was formed in any order after passing into the field or while at the houses, and further that when the command "charge" was given the men were in <no> order at all, "scattered around" being <illegible> <illegible> in his narrative, "the men at that time <largely> dismounted, some getting water at the bayou, some lying on the ground holding their horses"; and in answer to the question "in what order the squadron was formed while halting about the houses" says "in the greatest disorder." <Srgt F.> belongs to Capt. T's company and was at that time on the advanced guard. Private McConnell testifies "They (the men) all galloped up to the houses and scattered around, some looking in at the doors, others at the windows, some dismounted going to get water, some to light their pipes, some lying on the pommels of their saddles." <Srgt. Clark> says: "on arriving at the houses the squadron was in a perfect state of disorder, scattered to right and left, <illegible> of the men mounted, some dismounted, some getting water." Private Lavoisien says that when he arrived at the houses a crowd of men were pressing around Capt. T to look at and listen to the captured Mexican who was being questioned, but when ordered back they scattered about and <he> himself rode in around the houses, that some were getting water, some dismounted too, all these witnesses testify also that this was the state of the command <when> the order to charge was given. From this combination of direct and positive testimony it is clear that Capt. T is himself mistaken, that the statement in my report is totally and exactly correct, the men were "scattered in every direction" and probably Capt. T was so much engaged in his examination of the Mexican that the position and <arrangement> of his men escaped his attention. The last <in->accuracy which Capt. T points out is contained in the words, "Capt. T <turned> to the right and skirted the interior of the fence the men following him and it <consists> <ac>cording to Capt. T, only in the order in which the events occurred. He states that he first saw the squadron, or a portion of it, turn to the right and followed in order to rally them, then fully <illegible> the turning to the right, or in other words the turning to the right commencement of a retreat by both himself and the men at the time <stated> by me, and writes a "difference only as to the succession" in which the movement took place. From my position in rear it <was> at least possible that I did not note that success<ion> accurately and that Capt. T is correct. <Certainly enough> he fully believes himself so, or his statement would not <have> been made, but the evidence of Lieut. Kane and all the other witnesses on this point, shows clearly that they shared my error, if it was one, and considered her squadron, or part of it, as following Capt. T in turning to the right. In his official report Capt. T says that finding the numbers of the enemy too great to be <coped> with he "ordered a retreat." If the men were already retreating and his movement to the right was only to rally them, this order was certainly superfluous—it could only have been to those who like himself were <illegible> from the enemy, <and> as the evidence shows he himself was in advance the enemy all of the squadron who were together, the inference seeming almost irresistible in favor of the correct<ness> of my account, that Capt. T turned to the right and the men followed him, "the order he gave I did not <hear> but saw the retreat which followed" etc. The two statements do not in fact at all conflict with each other, and <agrees with> the testimony of Lieut. Kane, Srgts. Freeman and Clark, and of Private Lavoisien, it is evident that a portion of the men had turned off to the right even while Capt. T was <dashing> on toward the enemy, and another portion was a <short> distance in his rear, and that as Capt. T himself says that <he> only turned his head to the right, and did not turn entirely around, he saw no doubt only that portion which first turned and were behind me, while I saw only those who were following him. These, Capt. T expressly declares, are the only inaccuracies in my report, of these only one can be considered of any importance, and <illegible> is fully <illegible> from the charge by the direct and positive testimony of five witnesses.

I come now to that portion of <my> report which more than any other is open to mis-construction and which, as it is now easy for one to perceive, <is not> expressed with such minute and careful exactness, as <under> the circumstances would have been advisable. Permit me to <remind> you gentlemen that the <position> I occupied in making this report was utterly <strange> and <novel> -- that the excitement of the scene had not yet subsided and that never for an instant dreaming of the harsh, bitter, and uncharitable crit-icism and cavil to which any <language> would be subjected, I thought of no precaution against misconstruction as might arise from this. I say in my report that "foreseeing <it> I turned to the right and called upon the men to follow me." The language used by Col. Twiggs and Capt. May in their testimony <both> show how entirely, and for me how un-fortunately, this passage has been misconstrued. From the combined testimony of all the witnesses in the clearest and most positive form, it is evident that at the period to which this <phrase> refers, all form and order were lost, that the men were scattered in every direction each seeking his own safety, that the comd'g officer was nowhere to be seen, that only some dozen men were any where together, that nowhere was any attempt or effort at attack or resistance being made, and that my call to "follow me" so far from being addressed to any party of men who were following the comd'g officer in any direction, or <illegible> <illegible> his orders, was <illegible> only to some half a dozen <stragglers> who chanced to be near me, and to two or three others fallen in with afterwards in the bushes, after the comd'g officers had been carried away by his unmanageable horse and was no longer visible in the field. It may be he <illegible> that in a report which was to pass through the hands of the enemy I was not disposed to <visit upon> all these particu-lars, was not disposed to dwell at length and minutely upon the completeness of our sur-prise and the utter confusion of the rout, but took refuge in those vague generalities which are always exposed to misconstruction, and which can be rightfully understood only after all the circumstances are known. The details of these circumstances as now laid before the court shows that the twenty five men who finally surrendered, were not led by me in a body to the bank of the river, nor did they follow me there in obedience of any order of mine, <nor> less in opposition of any order or direction from Capt. T, but a number of them were there before I came, several joined me on the way, and <that> all I did was to rally and form as many of the stragglers and fugitives as could be formed with the intent of resistance to the last extreme or an honorable surrender. The remaining portion of my report, which relates to the effort made to escape by the river and the yielding myself and my men as prisoners, <illegible> when retreat and resistance were alike impossible and hopeless, is fully substantiated by the evidence of Srgt. Clark and Privates McConnell, Lavoisien, and Orr. I will not detain the court with a recapitulation of this evidence, but <turn> to the second point which I have sought to establish, the character of the ground on which the affair took place. The sketch placed <upon> the record of the court and <illegible> by all the witnesses will make this clearer than any verbal description. Lieut. Kane and several others testify that the main fence surrounding the plantation within which we were could not be leaped by any horses, that even the cross fences. tho' much lower, were <most> formidable obstacles, and the <ground> itself almost impracticable for cavalry. The third point "the disposition of the men at the time of the attack and their condition when the retreat commenced," has been <almost anticipated> in the remarks and evidence <from> the first.

It has been shown that no part of the company or squadron was formed in any kind of order, that no command was given them to form after they <galloped> by single file into the field, but no guard was placed in front of the plantation, or at the bars, that the command "charge" <from> Capt. T. was not succeeded by any order to form in any <manner>, but that, with the woods <yet> upon his <left>, with no thought apparently save to bring himself as soon as possible into contact with the enemy, he dashed forward and left the men to follow according to individual inclination or the speed of their horses. When the charge was made was in <this> manner, it is evident that the retreat which immediately followed would be, as the language of all the witnesses shows it, "confusion worse confounded", a flight in which all concert and discipline were lost, the horses beyond the control of the riders, the men thinking each of his individual safety, either heeding no orders or unable to obey them if heard. Capt. T. and Lieut. Kane both state that the order of the former "to halt and pull down the fence," which order Capt. T says was repeated by me was not obeyed. Capt. T was unable to stop even his own horse, and most of the men were in the same condition; a few moments afterwards we find Capt. T dashing against and unhorsing one of his own officers--a <cogent> proof how little at the time his course and direction were the result of his own volition; his own testimony shows that immediately after his horse fell on him--that he was unable to rise and saw no more of the squadron. <illegible> of the witnesses examined saw nothing <illegible> after the retreat commenced, and all state positively that they heard no orders given, no <party> were acting in concert to attack or to resist the enemy after that time, but each man was "taking care of himself as well as he could and supposed all the rest will doing the same." Lieut. Kane states "that he considered himself and every other man justified in seeking his safety by the best means in his power," such was the state of his command at the moment of attack and in the retreat. When I called upon the men to "follow me" then, and it seems that few if any heard the call, I was seeking only to rally some of the small number about that time in my sight and to <illegible> in the only direction which seemed to offer any hope of escape, namely to the river: followed at most by five or six, I took this course, found some others on the way, and on reaching the river bank was joined by several more until twenty five in all were collected there, the only body which had been assembled under the control of an officer since the retreat commenced.

Upon the last point, "my <own> conduct and bearing throughout the affair," I have refrained, influenced by emotions that I am sure the court will not misunderstand, from taking direct testimony from Lieut. Kane, and his it is not necessary for me to repeat. Upon a subject so delicate I prefer to leave the facts proven to take their own course to make their <own> impression upon the mind of the court, earnestly entreating them however, to recall any or all of these witnesses <in> my absence to examine them upon this point, since it is almost impossible for a soldier to give free and unembarrassed <evi>- dence in such a case in the presence of the officer concerned.

Having thus passed over all the ground covered by my report and touched with a brevity justified I trust by the clear consistent and positive character of the testimony, upon such points as seemed to me most important, I proceed to that part of my task which more than any other is painful and mortifying. I proceed to notice those imputations upon <my> conduct in this matter, which, while as one witness so truly stated, they have never attained the dignity of charges, have yet been whispered, <illegible>, and <dwelt> upon by those among whom I should have expected to find my warmest defense - the officers of my own Regt. The testimony of Capt. Larnard proves only the existence and repetition of such imputations; that of Col. Twiggs and Capt May shows their character and <impact> with sufficient clearness. They seem, as far as they present a tangible form, to resolve themselves into three <threads>.

1st of a contradiction between my official report and that of Capt. Thornton. 2nd of an alleged interference by me with Capt. T's orders, whereby a portion of the men were led away from him and diverted from his command; and 3rd, in my having surrendered too soon and before a sufficient number of men were killed and wounded. With regard to the first of these Capt. Thornton himself will probably be universally admitted the best judge and he says under oath, what is palpable indeed upon the face of the two docu- ments, that there is no discrepancy or contradictions between them; were other evidence required it would be supplied by Col. Twiggs, who bases this discrepancy upon assertions and expressions which are not to be found in my report at all. Upon the 2nd thread Col. Twiggs says Capt. Hardee "was thought censurable" in this, "that when Capt. Thornton gave orders for a charge Capt. Hardee gave different orders," and Capt. May, though with more circumlocution, makes the same assertion as coming from others and gives it as his own opinion also. <That>, upon the premises assumed, both these gentlemen are perfectly right, no officer worthy to hold a commission would deny. It would grieve me to suppose that <illegible> could think otherwise; the error is that these <illegible> are utterly with- out foundation in fact, as is most conclusively proved by the evidence before you. When Capt. Thornton gave the order to charge, Srgt. Clark, Privates McConnell and Lavoisien testify that I endeavored to get the men into some kind of order, directing them "to form or to form as well as they could," and the <illegible> of Lieut. Kane and others proved that the <order> was at once obeyed in my own person, as Capt T says that I upheld his order to "halt and pull down the fence" which was given to the most advanced and exposed faction of the command and Lieut. K testifies that I came up to him immediately after he was dismounted by Capt. T following on the same path with the captain. No other order to charge was given, by Capt. T or anyone else, nor did Capt. T's horse when he ran away take a direction which would have brought his <rider> in contact with the enemy, nor was he followed by any number of men. Lieut. K says "he was skirting the interior of the fence and was in a position from whence he could neither attack the enemy nor defend himself." It was not however until, according to all the evidence, Capt. Thornton was no longer visible upon the field, that I made the effort to rally and lead to the river the few stragglers whom I saw around me, and this effort it would seem to be, which, described in my report in general, perhaps rather vague terms, has been made the subject of such misrepresentations, of a charge so shameful and unworthy as a desertion of my comd'g officer. Most sincerely do I hope that no other motive save an ardent and sincere <care> for the honor of the Regt and the service has activated those who have so ingeniously <found> the worst of all possible explanations for that which no doubt requires none. There are minds so delicate and exquisitely sensitive that even the very <illegible> <illegible> drives them into extravagance. No doubt it <was> by such I have been so harshly and so <rashly judged>.

The third imputation against me is of having surrendered too soon and before a sufficient number of the men were killed or wounded. The evidence proves that we were surrounded by a party of some two thousand men; that we were shut up within an enclosure which our horses could neither leap nor break down, that an effective charge was therefore impracticable, and that the enemy by lining the hedge with his infantry could have picked us off at leisure and with <scarce> a possibility of resistance on our part. When I had rallied the twenty five men upon the bank of the river, I had no doubt that all the remainder of the squadron were killed or wounded and that would have been a <proposition> with which the most blood-thirsty fire-<eaters> could scarce find fault and which might surely justify the survivors, scarce half armed as they were, all retreat cut off and all resistance hopeless, in surrendering themselves as prisoners of war.

I shall now gentlemen without further comment place my case in your hands. I have earnestly desired not to <try> the patience with which you have heard me by a single superfluous word and have therefore <illegible> much which feeling might have <illegible> prompted. <More> will I am sure pardon me for entreating, that you make use of the power placed in your hands by the order convening the court, to render your verdict full complete and comprehensive -- to express your opinion of my conduct, upon all the circumstances of this affair as connected with myself, and upon the <imputations> which have been made against me, in terms so clear and precise as to free me forever from the <breath> of censure as to remove every <shade> from my <illegible> reputation. I desire no better criterion than the feeling which has place in your own breasts, and in the <illegible> of that honor which to the soldier is the <illegible> of life. I ask you to do me justice.

Respectfully submitted
W. J. Hardee
Capt 2d Dragoons

##

APPENDIX E

Transcript, Court-Martial of Capt. Seth B. Thornton, Matamoros, Mexico, July 1846

What follows is a typescript of the National Archives file of the Thornton court-martial. The cover page and archival notations were disregarded. For legibility, ampersands were rendered with "and." The original line breaks and page breaks were not preserved. Otherwise the author has tried to capture all the original text and formatting of the file, including the original spelling, abbreviations, and formatting, which included underlining, right-justification, left-justification, and centering. All the quotation marks shown were in the original.

Basically, the file was in better physical shape than the Hardee file (as mentioned in the previous Appendix D) and all the text was eventually recovered except for one signature.

There were two appended documents in the file, and they are included at the end as they were in the original:

Thornton's defense summation, labeled D (although there was no A, B, or C).

A hand-drawn map.

The text refers to reference letters that are on the map—and to some that cannot be found on the map. There are also letters on the map that aren't referenced. North is down. There was no scale, but the huts were elsewhere described as 200 yards from the barred gate on the west side of the field. The author's edited version of the map appears in Chapter 4.

Transcript text follows:

<u>First Case</u>

The trial of Captain Seth B. Thornton, Second Regiment US Dragoons.

Proceedings of a General Court Martial trial held at Matamoros, Mexico, by virtue of the following order:

War Department,
Adjutant General's Office
Washington, June 12, 1846.
General Order No. 20

By direction of the President of the United States, a General Court Martial will be assembled in the camp of the Army of Occupation, at such time as the General in Command may appoint, for the trial of Col. William Whistler, of the 4th Regiment of Infantry, and Cap. Seth B. Thornton, of the 2nd Regiment of Dragoons, and such business as may be brought before it.

Detail for the Court
1. Bvt. Brig. Gen. W. J. Worth
2. Col. W. Gates, 3rd Artillery
3. Lt. Col. Henry Whiting, Deputy Quartermaster General
4. Lt. Col. J. Garland, 4th Infantry
5. Bvt. Lt. Col. T. Childs, 3rd Artillery
6. Bvt. Lt. Col. W. G. Belknap, 8th Infantry
7. Lt. Col. H. Wilson, 1st Infantry
8. Major P. H. Craig, Medical Department
9. Major W. W. Lear, 3rd Infantry
10. Bvt. Major W. M. Graham, 4th Infantry
11. Bvt. Major J. Dimmacho, 1st Artillery
12. Bvt. Major G. W. Allen, 4th Infantry
13. Bvt. Major J. J. Abercrombie, 1st Infantry

Capt. C. F. Smith, 2nd Artillery, is appointed the Judge Advocate of the Court.

"II Should any of the officers named in the detail be prevented from attending at the time and place hereafter appointed, the court will nevertheless proceed to continue the business before it, provided the number of members present be not less than the nine minimum prescribed by law.

By order:
(Signed) R. Jones
Adg. Gen.

Head Quarter Army of Occupation
Matamoros, July 10, 1846

Orders, No. 84

The General Court Martial instituted in "General Order No. 20," will meeting at 10 o'clock am tomorrow in the room provided for its sessions by the QM's Dept.
By order of Major Gen. Taylor
(Signed) W. W. S. Bliss
Asst. Adg. Gen.

First Day

Matamoros, Mexico
Saturday, 10 of the clock am
July 11, 1846

The court met pursuant to the above order. Present:

1. Bvt. Brig. Gen. W. J. Worth
2. Lt. Col. J. Garland, 4th Inf.
3. Bvt. Lt. Col. J. Childs, 4th Art.
4. Bvt. Lt. Col. W. G. Belknap, 8th Inf.
5. Lt. Col. H. Wilson, 1st Inf.
6. Major W. W. Lear, 3rd Inf.
7. Bvt. Major W. M. Graham, 4th Inf.
8. Bvt. Major G. W. Allen, 4th Inf.
9. Bvt. Major J. J. Abercrombie, 1st Inf.
10. _____
11. _____
12. _____
13. _____

Capt. C. F. Smith, 2nd Art., Judge Advocate

The court then proceeded to the trial of Capt. Seth B. Thornton, of the 2nd Regiment of Dragoons, who having heard the "General Orders" was asked if he had any objections to either of the members named herein, to which he replied in the negative. The court and the Judge Advocate were then duly sworn in presence of the accused.

Capt. Thornton asked for, and obtained permission from the court, for Bvt. Capt. Barbour, 3rd Inf., and 1st Lt. Bragg, 3rd Art., to attend as his counsel. He was then arraigned with the following charges:

"Charge 1st, Neglect of Duty.

"Specification: In this, that Capt. S. B. Thornton, 2nd Dragoons, being in command of a squadron of said regiment, detached from the camp opposite Matamoros, by order of Bvt. Brig. Gen. Taylor, Commanding, Army of Occupation, to watch the movement of the enemy, and to ascertain if he had crossed the Rio Grande in force, did omit the necessary and customary precautions, to secure his command against surprise, and did suffer it to be ambuscaded, and entirely cut off by a large force of the Mexican Army—this on the left bank of the Rio Grande, near the Rancho "Las Rusias," and in or about the 25th of April, 1846.

"Charge 2d, Disobedience of Orders.

"Specification: In this, that Capt. S. B. Thornton, 2nd Dragoons, being in command of a squadron of said regiment, detached from the camp opposite Matamoros, under instructions from Bvt. Brig. Gen. Z. Taylor, Commanding, Army of Occupation, in the following words and figures, to wit:

"Head Quarters, Army of Occupation
"Camp near Matamoros, Texas
"April 24th, 1846

"Sir:
"The Commanding General directs that you proceed with your squadron up the river as far as 9 leagues, examining the country and river carefully to ascertain if the enemy has crossed to this side. Should you discern that he has crossed and in too great force for you to cope with successfully, you will return at once to head quarters and report to the Commanding General. In case you should see no signs of crossing as far as 9 leagues, you will likewise return and report the result of your examination. The General desires that you move with the utmost caution, keeping out advanced and flank guards, and taking the greatest care not to be drawn into an ambuscade. You will hold yourself ready to cut through any armed party that may be in your way.

"I am, Sir, very respectfully
"Your obd. servant
(Signed) "W. W. S. Bliss
"Asst. Adj. Gen.

"Capt. S. B. Thornton,
"2nd Dragoons,
"Command Squadron"

did, in violation of said instructions, and of verbal instructions of the same import, communicated to him by Bvt. Brig, Gen. Taylor, aforesaid, on the 24th of April, 1846, omit the necessary and customary precautions, to secure his command against surprise and did suffer it to be ambuscaded, and entirely cut off, by a large force of the Mexican Army.

This on the left bank of the Rio Grande, near the Rancho "Las Rusias." and in or about the 25th of April, 1846.

(Signed) "Z. Taylor
"Bvt. Brig. Gen. US Army"

To which charges and specifications the accused pleaded "Not Guilty."

Bvt. Capt. W. W. S. Bliss, a witness for the prosecution, having been duly sworn, says:

"On the 24th of April last, as well as I recollect, after dark, I was directed by the Commanding General to draw up certain instructions, for the guidance of Capt. Thornton for the conduct of an expedition of the left bank of the Rio Grande. Those instructions are copied in the Specifications to the 2d Charge, which I have just heard read, and those delivered to Capt. Thornton in my office on the same evening.

"I have no recollection of hearing any verbal instructions to Capt. Thornton by the Commanding General."

Q by J. A.... "Do you know the usual name or designation of the Village or Rancho beside the river about 9 leagues from Fort Brown?"

Answer: "To the best of my belief it is known by the name "'Las Rusias.'"

The witness retires.

Bvt. Maj. Gen. Z. Taylor, US Army, a witness for the prosecution, having been duly sworn in, says:

"About the time specified Col. Twiggs was at my tent and I directed him to have a command of dragoons detailed, which was done, and Capt. Thornton reported to me for orders. On handing him his orders, I impressed upon him the necessity of moving with utmost caution: That his object was to ascertain if the reports regarding the Mexican force and its position were true. My object in sending the command was information: That if he met with a small party he might capture them, but if in force to avoid them: That he would keep out a small front and flank guard, and thoroughly examine every place with a few men, whenever there was a possibility of an ambush being made before he committed his command. That it would be better to rush and sacrifice a few than the whole, but should he get surrounded he would cut his way through and return to camp."

Q by Accused… "In your verbal instructions did you not direct me to ascertain if the enemy had artillery?"

Witness…."It is possible but I do not recollect having done so."

Q by Accused…. "Did you not say to me, 'I shall expect you back by 12 o'clock tomorrow'?"

Witness… "Yes, perhaps I might."

The witness retires.

Surgeon P. H. Craig, Medical Staff, a witness for the Prosecution, having been duly sworn, says:

"It was near Fort Brown, then in construction, towards the end of April last, I heard Genl. Taylor direct Capt. Thornton to be particularly careful in his movement up the river, and not to fall into an ambuscade. He directed him to keep out advanced parties and to be very careful."

Q by Accused… "Were you present during the whole of the interview between Genl. Taylor and Capt. Thornton?"

Witness…. "Only a part of it, at Capt. Waggamon's tent."

The witness retires.

Capt. W. J. Hardee, 2nd Dragoon, witness for the prosecution, having been duly sworn, says:

"Late in the afternoon of the 24th of April last I rec'd orders to get my company ready to proceed up the river with Capt. Thornton, as Genl. Taylor had rec'd information that the Mexicans had crossed above in strength.

"Capt. Thornton's command, consisting of his company and my own, left the camp opposite Matamoros about 9 o'clock at night. Before leaving Capt. Thornton gave me instructions to remain in rear of the column. Lt. Mason was with me. We proceeded up the river with Chipito as our guide. After proceeding several miles Capt. Thornton asked me if I knew where there was any place suitable to rest for an hour or two. I told him there was a convenient place about 15 miles, at a Rancho. When we arrived there he asked me about the locality of the place, and what dispositions it would be necessary to make to prevent a surprise. I told him to place a sentinel up and down the road, 2 or 300 yards. No one would then approach without his knowing it: this was done.

"Before daylight the next morning the march was resumed. I do not know if there was any advance guard—it was impossible for me to see from my position in the rear. There was no rear guard and no flankers, to my knowledge. The condition of the woods, however, was such as to be impracticable for horse riders on both sides of the road, and, in most places, even for footmen. In proceeding upwards Capt. Thornton made constant enquiries if the enemy had crossed, and I believe he was invariably told they had, but all spoke from rumor. After we had marched about 10 miles from the place where we had halted, he came upon a ranch where there were 3 or 4 Mexicans. Capt. Thornton went forward and questioned them with Chipito, from what I could learn these men stated that the enemy had crossed in force, and Chipito refused to go any further. After this the march was resumed without him, and Lieut. Mason was detached from the rear to the front, I did not know for what purpose. About 3 miles from this place the command came across a large field, of which this [see accompanying paper marked "A"] is a rough sketch. Capt. Thornton advanced to penetrate to the houses in the field by the rear [at X], for which purpose he made a countermarch which threw me up the river, i.e., in front.

"The command having halted I went to Capt. Thornton to ask him something about his arrangements, and he told me to repair again to my position, as he did not know how soon we might be attacked. After returning Srgt. Clark of my company (C) reported to me that a horseman had made his appearance from the chaparral, and that as soon as he saw the command he immediately disappeared. I reported this to Capt. Thornton as he was returning from an unsuccessful attempt to penetrate the field. He asked what direction he had taken and a small path was pointed out.

"The command then entered into the chaparral at the point C. After penetrating 3 or 400 yards without discovering the enemy, the column countermarched and resumed the old route around the field.

"The next time I saw Capt. Thornton after this countermarch, he was in the field between the draw bars and the huts [D and L], and I saw also some Mexicans flying from the houses; I do not know if they were armed, I believe they were not. Into this field the whole command entered in single file. When I got up to the houses the command was scattered around, some looking in at the doors, some at the windows. After the lapse of about 5 minutes I saw Capt. Thornton conversing with an old Mexican. I went up to where he was. Immediately after this the cry was given that the Mexicans were coming. I looked towards the bars and I saw footmen and horsemen rushing towards them in a run, coming from the front, i.e., up the river.

"As soon as the cry of alarm was given Capt. Thornton gave the command 'Charge' and himself dashed off in a full gallop. I repeated the command and thought I saw all the men started when I dashed off myself. When I got about midway between the bars and the huts I looked for Capt. Thornton and saw him near the bars in front of the enemy. The enemy had possession of the bars, and the next I saw of Capt. Thornton he turned to the right and was skirting the interior of the chaparral fence. By the time I got up to the place I last mentioned about 100 infantry had got into the field; had formed into line perpendicular to the fence and were shooting at our men.

"The firing of the infantry caused our horses to shy, and the men broke off about midway [at O] between the bars and the houses and towards the fence.

"When the retreat commenced the men were in a complete state of disorder. The horses were made frantic by the firing, which was continued by the infantry, and by the horsemen who were around the chaparral fence.

"This field was enclosed by a high chaparral fence, wholly impracticable for a horseman, and lastly on the river. Within this field there were also three cross-fences, very difficult for a horse to jump, the whole field comprising about 300 acres. The cross-fences ran perpendicular to the main fence, in length about 40 yards, and resting upon a Morass situated between them and the river. The Morass was very boggy.

"Immediately after the retreat the squadron fell into the hands of the enemy, 46 being taken prisoner. I do not know the number we started with but believe it was between 50 and 60.

"The road through which we passed in almost its entire length is a perfect defile, surrounded by thick chaparral on each side, and so narrow in some places as to render it difficult for a horseman to pass."

Q by J. A..... "What precautions were taken, if any, to prevent surprise, before the squadron passed the bars, and after?"

Witness... "I do not know of any."

Q by J. A.... "Do you know if any picket or sentinel was in advance of the bars, up the river?"

Witness... "I do not."

Q by J. A.... "Where was your position on entering the bars?"

Witness... "In the rear."

Q by J. A…."Would you have known if a sentinel or vidette had been thrown in advance of the bars?"

Witness… "When I went in I might not have known it, but certainly would have known afterwards by his being driven in by the enemy, had one been posted."

Q by J. A…. "Was a guard or sentinel placed at the bars to secure them after the squadron had passed into the field?"

Witness… "No."

Q by J. A…."State more particularly the condition of the squadron after it had entered the plantation—in reference to battle array?"

Witness… "As I have stated in my narration the command was scattered about, some of the men looking in at the houses; some getting water from the river or bayou, a considerable portion was dismounted—how many I do not know. No part of it was united to receive or repel an attack."

Q by J. A…."What is the name of the place where the affair occurred"

Witness…. "I have heard it called 'Caracita.' It was about three miles below La Rosies where the enemy crossed."

Q by J. A…."How long after the squadron entered the plantation before it was attacked?"

Witness… "About 5 minutes after I got to the houses."

Q by J. A…. "What is the distance between the bars and the houses?"

Witness… "About 200 yards."

Q by J. A…."What was the force of the enemy?"

Witness… "About 2,000 men. I make this estimate as much from what I saw afterwards as from what I saw at the time of the attack."

Q by J. A…. "What was the disposition of the enemy's force when the squadron was attacked and immediately thereafter?"

Witness… "When I first saw the enemy, horsemen and footmen were seen running pell-mell for the bars; when I next saw them they were inside of the field, in a line perpendicular to the fence and facing the road from the bars to the houses; horsemen surrounded the exterior fence, and fired upon us as we were retreating around it."

Q by J. A…. "Describe the manner in which the squadron passed the bars—whether in order or otherwise?"

Witness… "It passed in single file, in a regular manner."

Q by J. A…. "Were there any indications of any enemy whilst the squadron was moving around the plantation?"

Witness… "When we entered the chaparral [at C] there was a slight rain, sufficient to obliterate the tracks we had made on the road, and on coming out I examined the road and found that a horseman had passed up and down the road whilst we were in the chaparral. This was suspicious, but I do not know that Capt. Thornton knew of it.

"Some 2 or 3 horsemen were seen in the field, but they seemed more like peasants than soldiers."

Q by J. A…. "Have you any reason to believe that Capt. Thornton suspected the existence of the enemy near him whilst skirting the plantation?"

Witness… "No other reason than what I have previously mentioned, that, when he endeavored to penetrate the field by the rear, he ordered me back to my position, stating he did not know how long it would be before we were attacked."

"Capt. Thornton, however, stated to me at Matamoros, since then, that this was only a precautionary measure, for he did not believe the enemy had crossed."

Q by J. A…. "What is the distance from Fort Brown to Caracito—so called?"

Witness… "About 28 miles."

Q by J. A…. "Was the chaparral so thick throughout the march as to prevent flankers from being used at any time; and was there any advance or rear guard, at any time, during the march?"

Witness… "The country through which we passed was so thick as to render flankers impossible at any time. From my position in the rear it was impossible to see the advance guard if there was one. There was no rear guard."

Q by J. A.... "Was the command under Capt. Thornton 'entirely cut off'?"

Witness... "I do not know if any escaped except Capt. Thornton, who was subsequently taken prisoner; and a private by the name of James who was brought in 2 or 3 days afterwards."

The witness retired.

2d Lieut. E. K. Kane, 2d Dragoons, a witness for the prosecution, having been duly sworn, says:

"I commanded the first platoon of Capt. Thornton's squadron on the 25th of April last. I was with the squadron when it was attacked by the Mexicans between 25 and 30 miles from Fort Brown. This sketch [accompanying paper marked "A"] conveys a generally correct idea of the place of attack."

Q by J. A.... "In what order did the squadron pass the bar into the plantation; and was it in confusion on the other side?"

Witness... "It passed in single file and in good order."

Q by J. A.... "During the march of the squadron from the Camp of the Army to Caracita, what precautions were taken by the accused, if any, to prevent surprise?"

Witness... "Previous to our leaving camp there was an advanced guard under a non-comm'd officer, about 150 yards in front. This, with directions to keep silent and prevent the jingling of spurs were the precautions observed from the time of leaving the camp until that of attack. The orders to keep silence and to prevent noise were frequently repeated and passed from front to rear, from man to man. About 2 miles from Caracita the advance guard was increased and placed under the charge of Lieut. Mason."

Q by J. A.... "Where was the advance guard when the squadron entered the plantation?"

Witness... "The squadron closed up accidentally on the advance guard at the bars, owing to the thickness of the chaparral and the wandering of the road, both entered the plantation together.

"The advance guard had orders to keep one-fourth of a mile ahead. Had I been able to see that the advance guard had halted I would have halted the head of the squadron.

"Capt. Thornton was in the field at the time."

<u>Q by J. A.</u>…. "After the squadron entered the plantation, was a guard or sentinel placed at the bars, or in advance of them i.e., up the river; or were any precautions taken to present a surprise?"

<u>Witness</u>… "No."

<u>Q by J. A.</u>…. "Describe the condition of the squadron after it had entered the plantation with reference to its battle array?"

<u>Witness</u>… "We entered the bars and judged to capture a flying enemy; Mexicans having been seen at the houses about 200 yards from the bars. The advance guard was in front of the squadron, Capt. <u>Thornton</u> leading. After I got up to the houses at the head of the squadron, Capt. <u>Thornton</u> was there and turned to the squadron and said, 'I did not want you all to come in here', as there were 3 or 4 there then in pursuit of the Mexicans. He then reined up, the squadron coming up together, and Capt. <u>Hardee</u> and myself and several of the men went off about 20 yards to our left to examine the houses, we being between the houses and the river.

"I then returned to the main body of the squadron and after getting a drink from a man whom I had directed to get off his horse for that purpose, Sgt. <u>Tredo</u>, who was on my left hallooed to me '<u>There are the Mexicans Lieutenant</u>'; which was carried through the squadron immediately.

"Capt. <u>Thornton</u> who was in front of the squadron i.e. farther from the bars than the rest of the squadron, galloped across to the rear of the squadron nearest the bars and gave the command 'Charge'; which was immediately executed by Sgt. <u>Tredo</u> and myself.

"When the command 'Charge' was given the command was not in any regular formation. I thought generally the whole of the squadron dashed ahead when the command 'Charge' was given, though I think some few were dismounted.

"At the time the command 'Charge' was given the squadron occupied a space of about 100 yards around. Some of the men were getting water, one or two, some were at the houses, perhaps one or two also; they were generally talking and laughing with each other at the Mexicans having fled."

<u>Q by J. A.</u>…. "Were there any indications of the enemy before you entered the plantation?"

<u>Witness</u>… "Some distance before getting to the bars we came to the path marked "C"; one of the men, Sgt. <u>Clark</u>, reported that he had seen a Mexican going down this path. This was after going to the corner of the field at "K", countermarching and returning to the point "B". When we came back to the point "C" Capt. <u>Thornton</u> went down the path

to examine it; he came to me and said about 500 horsemen had gone down this path. He then went down the path, we followed expecting to come up with the Mexicans. After we had gone about a mile and a half we came to a marshy prairie; we then returned and went around the plantation and through the bars.

"After Capt. Thornton examined the path he said to me 'We shall have to cut our way back'; and gave me particular instructions, what to do in that event."

Q by J. A…. "Was the attacking party large or small?"

Witness… "Large, about 2,000. This estimate was formed during the attack, and was confirmed by after observations."

Q by J. A…. "Was the squadron 'entirely cut off'?"

Witness… "It was: either killed, wounded, or taken prisoner."

Q by J. A…. "What was the character of the country, on either side of the road, on which you marched from the Camp opposite Matamoros to the point at which you were attacked?"

Witness… "It was thick chaparral; the road was very crooked following the windings of the river."

The witness retired.

Sergeant George Lenz of Company B, 2d Dragoons, a witness for the prosecution, being duly sworn in says:

"I had charge of the advance guard of Capt. Thornton's squadron when it left the Camp of the Army on the 24th of April last and until the guide left us the next morning. I then belonged to Capt. Thornton's company (F). The advance consisted of two privates and myself. There was with us a guide, Chipito.

"After the guide left us the advance guard consisted of about 10 or 12 men commanded by Lt. Mason; I going with it as interpreter.

Q by J. A…. "In what order was the squadron after it had halted in the plantation?"

Witness… "Twelve or 14 men were dismounted getting water; and some were listening to what the citizen, whom we had caught, was saying. Another party was searching the houses with Lt. Kane. No part of the squadron was drawn up in line of battle: when the command "Charge" was given by Capt. Thornton the squadron was in the same condition I have just described. The squadron had closed upon the advance when it entered the bars, and mixed in with it."

The witness retired.

At half past 2 of the clock P.M. the court was adjourned to meet at 10 of the clock A.M. tomorrow.

Second Day

Sunday, 10 of the clock AM
July 12, 1846

The court meets pursuant to adjournment.

Present

1. Brig. Gen. Worth
2. Lt. Col. Garland
3. Lt. Col. Childs
4. Lt. Col. Belknap
5. Lt. Col. Wilson
6. Major Lear
7. Major Graham
8. Major Allen
9. Major Abercrombie

Capt. C. F. Smith, Judge Advocate

Capt. Thornton in attendance

Private James Orr, of Co. F., 2d Dragoons, a witness for the prosecution, was duly sworn in, but it appearing on the commencement of his examination that he was somewhat intoxicated he was directed to withdraw and was placed in confinement.

Private William McConnell, of Co. C, 2d Dragoons, a witness for the prosecution, having been duly sworn in, says:

"I was with Capt. Thornton's squadron when it was captured in April last. My position was about 2/3 in rear of the squadron. It went into the plantation in single file and rode in regularly. Capt. Thornton rode in first, then a few men—a part of the advance guard—followed him into the field. I think I heard him say to Sgt. Freeman to follow him, who, I believe, was in the advance guard.

"After riding in and calling for Sgt. Freeman, as I believe, he then turned and beckoned in the remainder of the squadron to follow him, as I believe: they did so at all events."

Q by J. A.... "Describe the condition of the squadron after it had halted in the field, whether in line of battle or otherwise?"

Witness... "When it rode up some of them dismounted to get some water; some to get some fire to light their pipes; others rode around to the doors looking in to see what was to be seen. They were in that condition until the alarm was given. There were a great many dismounted; over one half of them I should think. None were drawn up in line of battle. The men were scattered around in a space of 200 yards I suppose."

Q by J. A.... "Was any guard or sentinel placed at the bars after the squadron entered?"

Witness... "None that I saw, that is when I entered."

Q by Accused... "Were any of the men of the squadron at the houses beyond the reach of command from the position which Capt. Thornton himself occupied?"

Witness... "I do not believe there was."

Q by Accused... "When the cry of alarm was given and Capt. Thornton ordered the charge, did the squadron assemble rapidly and charge in a body?"

Witness... "No they did not. A few men who were around where I was standing with my horse advanced toward the enemy with Capt. Thornton, who was leading the way. I was close to Capt. Thornton myself and did not see who was in my rear. I did not see what was doing in my rear I was so far in the advance."

Q by Counsl. ... "Did you hear any order or permission given to dismount, or break early, after the command reached the houses?"

Witness... "No, I did not."

The witness retired.

The testimony for the prosecution closed here.

Capt. W. J. Hardee, 2d Dragoons, recalled as a witness for the defense, says:

Q. by Accused… "Did you or not hear me give instructions to the squadron to remain on the alert, during the rest at night, and to hold their bridles ready to mount and move in case of alarm?"

Witness… "I did in the night of the 24th."

Q by Accused… "When informed that the enemy was within a mile and a half of us, at the ranch when the guide left us, did I not order the command to sling and load their carbines, examine the priming of their pistols and take off and strap their great coats and be ready for action as the enemy was near?"

Witness… "I do not recollect that he did. The order may have been given, however, without my knowing it."

Q. by Accused… "Had the squadron kept at the distance of a quarter of a mile from the advance guard would it have entered the field at all?

Witness… "I think the enemy would have come upon it before the squadron entered the field, according to the usual rate of travel."

Q by Accused… "Did you hear any order for the squadron to advance after it halted at the bars?"

Witness… "I did not. Had such an order been given I would not have heard it being at such a distance from the head of the column."

Q by Accused… "How was I engaged from the time you saw me in the field and to the time of ordering the charge?"

Witness… "When I first saw Capt. Thornton he was between the bars and the houses; I supposed he was taking measures to pursue and capture the Mexicans who had fled from the houses. After my arrival at the houses he seemed to be anxiously occupied in finding someone with whom to communicate. An old man was brought to him and he was busily engaged in questioning him when the cry of alarm was given."

Q by Accused… "About what hour was it when the squadron entered the field where it was captured?"

Witness… "I may not be able to come within one or two hours of the time. I think it may have been between 9 and 10 of the clock AM."

Q by Accused… "Was the loss of my squadron in your opinion owing to its entrance into the field, or must it necessarily have been cut off in any attempt to return to camp?"

Witness… "From the nature of the country through which we passed, and information I subsequently derived from Mexican officers, of which there could be no doubt, the squadron would in my opinion have been entirely cut to pieces if it had not gone into the field."

Q by Accused… "Did you or not hear the Mexican officers say, whilst in Matamoros, or on your way thither, after the capture of the squadron, that they had known of our movement, and had already gained our rear before we reached the field?"

Witness… "After our capture I heard one or more Mexican officers say that their spies knew of our departure the moment we left camp: that they had spied upon us during our whole route: that Genl. Torrejon received information of our departure before 1 o'c that night: that they had persons on the road to point out our way. One of those persons, who was particularly officious left us when our guide did; he was afterwards recognized in uniform at our capture; and that when entered into the field they had 500 Cavalry, besides 150? Indians, in our rear."

Q by the Accused… "In view of the darkness of the night and the difficulties of the road, might not the rear of my command been easily gained by an enemy, well acquainted with the country, without the possibility of my knowing it?"

Witness… "I do not consider it necessary for the night to have done so, they could have done it in daytime."

Q by Accused… "Was it not your impression that our guide had betrayed us?"

Witness… "It was not."

The witness retired.

2nd Lt. E. K. Kane, 2d Dragoons, recalled as a witness for the defense, says:

Q by Accused… "Did you hear my instructions to the squadron at the time of halting for a rest in the night of the 24th? If so state the precautions I took to prevent a surprise?"

Witness… "I heard the commander of the squadron give instructions to Sgt. Smith, I think, the senior sergeant of the squadron, to place a sentinel, some hundred yards at each end of the road from the yard where we halted. He also directed that the men hold their horses by the bridle, which order I repeated to them myself."

Q by Accused… "When informed that the enemy was within a mile and a half of us, at the ranch where the guide left us; did I or not order my command to sling and load their carbines, examine the priming of their pistols, and take off and strap their great coats and to be ready for action, as the enemy was near?"

Witness… "He did."

Q by Accused… "Before reaching the bars of the field do you or not remember my ordering Lt. Mason with the advance guard to reconnoiter the field and the river bank, and my instructions to him, together with the position of the squadron at that time?"

Witness… "At the time Lt. Mason was placed in command of the advance guard, when it had been increased to 10 men and a non-com'd officer, he was ordered to keep about a quarter of a mile in advance of the squadron, if he came up with the enemy or any portion of them to fire on them and retire immediately."

"After we counter-marched to the lower end of the field—down the river—the squadron was halted in the road at the point "B", which I suppose is about 200 yards from the river."

"Capt. Thornton and the advance guard then went to the river, to the point where the fence intersected it, for the purpose of reconnoitering, as I supposed.

"I do not recollect any other instructions than those I have stated."

Q by Accused… "What were my particular instructions to you when I informed you of my belief that we should have to cut our way back to camp?"

Witness… "His instructions were: to keep as near him as possible with the head of the squadron, that he would hack his way through the enemy and I was to follow him to prevent the opening he might make from being closed, whether he fell or not."

Q by Accused… "Was I at the head of my squadron exercising the immediate command thereof at any time after it had closed with the advance guard at the bars and previous to the time of giving the command and order to "Charge?"

Witness… "He was not."

Q by Accused… "Did you hear any order from me for the squadron to advance after it had closed on the advance guard at the bars?"

Witness… "I did not hear any order. The squadron moved when he beckoned to advance."

Q by Accused... "How was I occupied when the squadron entered the field—what was my position with reference to the squadron when it halted—was I facing to or from it at the time of the alarm and charge—when was my occupation from the entrance of the squadron to the time of the charge?"

Witness... "When the squadron entered the field he was apparently going to the houses to get information as I supposed from some Mexicans who were at the houses."

"When it halted he was about 20 to 30 yards in advance of it engaged in conversation with a Mexican."

"He was facing from it."

"He was occupied the most of the time in talking to the Mexican. The rest of the time he was with the advance guard in pursuit of the enemy who was flying."

Q by Accused... "Was any order, authority, or permission given by me for the squadron to break ranks, to disperse, or for men to dismount?"

Witness... "There was not."

Q by Accused... "From my occupation at the time was it at all probable that the condition of the squadron came under my observation?"

Witness... "I didn't think it was."

Q by Accused... "Had the squadron kept its distance in rear of the advance guard would it have entered the field at all?"

Witness... "It would not."

Q by Accused... "What was your position in the squadron in reference to its commander, and your means of observing his condition and movement; compared to those of other officers of the squadron?"

Witness... "I was in command of the first platoon and therefore at the head of the squadron, and most of the time with the commanding officer, whose position is at the head of the squadron, i.e., from the time we attacked."

"My position was such as to enable me to know more of his movements than any other person of the squadron."

Q by Accused… "Do you or not believe that we were betrayed by our guide?"

Witness… "I did believe we were."

Q by Accused… "Did you or not learn after our capture that the enemy had full information of our movement and strength as early as one o'clock on the night of the 24th, and that at the time of our entering the field they had gained our rear with a large force?"

Witness… "I did hear so from many officers of Genl. Ampudia's staff; and that they had gained our rear with 500 Cavalry and 150 Indians."

Q by Accused… "Were you or not of the opinion that every man must have fallen had we not been captured in the field?"

Witness… "I was and I am of that opinion."

Q by Cousl… "State the grounds of your belief that the guide was treacherous."

Witness… "I believe so in the first place from the fact that when we stopped in the night of the 24th he left the command and was absent about an hour. The next morning he left the main trail we had followed up to this time and went through the woods for several miles to the left of the road. When we came up to the houses where our guide left us his conversation with the three men that were there was in a whisper and it was a long conversation—5 to 10 minutes. He then told the commander of the squadron he would not go any farther with him, that the Mexicans would cut his throat. Afterwards—some days—I don't know how long—he was seized by the Mexicans and pardoned by Genl. Arista. This I was told by Col. Moreno of the Mexican Army."

Q by Cousl…"You have stated your belief that the squadron would have been cut off in any event; state where the squadron was when you first entertained that belief."

Witness… "The squadron was in the field and had been and was still engaged with the enemy, i.e., the firing was going on. The Cavalry and Infantry had all passed me; I had seen the whole of them."

Q by Cousl… "When the squadron halted in the field, did Capt. Thornton give any direction for it to reform?"

Witness… "He did not."

Q by Cousl… "Have you any reason to believe that at the time the guide left you the enemy had gained your rear?"

<u>Witness</u>… "I know now from the fact that we afterward found their trail and examined it, which was leading to our rear. And we were afterward told (when prisoners) by Mexican Officers that they had gained our rear in force that night."

The witness retired.

The testimony of the Defense closed here.

The Accused requested of the Court until 10 o'clock on Wednesday morning next to prepare his defense, which request was granted,

At 1/2 past of the clock the court was adjourn to meet at 10 of the clock tomorrow morning.

Third Day

10 of the clock AM, Monday,
July 13, 1846
The court met pursuant to adjournment. The Court and the Judge Advocate present as on yesterday.

After the transaction of business unconnected with the case, the Court, at 10 minutes on the clock, was adjourned to meet at 10 of the clock AM on Wednesday, the 15th inst.

Fourth Day

10 of the clock AM, Wednesday,
July 15, 1846

The court met pursuant to adjournment. Present:

1. Brig. Gen. Worth
2. Lt. Col. Garland
3. Lt. Col. Childs
4. Lt. Col. Belknap
5. Lt. Col. Wilson

6. Major Lear
7. Major Graham
8. Major Allen
9. Major Abercrombie

Capt. C. F. Smith, Judge Advocate

Capt. Thornton in attendance

The Accused by his counsel then read the court the following Defense:

[see accompanying paper marked "D"]

The court was then cleared and the whole of the foregoing proceedings read; after which, and upon mature deliberation, the following decision was had:

<u>Finding</u>

On the <u>Specification</u> of the First Charge: In regard to this specification the Court is of opinion, that the Accused took the necessary and customary precautions, in all respects performed his duty as a commander, to the period of time when the troops entered the field referred to in the testimony: but that he omitted thereafter, on discovering the disarray of his command after it had closed up and halted, to put it in order of battle; which omission does not find sufficient excuse in the special engagement of the accused at the moment, or the brief space intervening between the halt and attack: that the squadron was cut off; but in the opinion of the court not as a consequence of any want of precaution, nor even of the condition of the troops when attacked, as above noted: And do therefore pronounce him <u>Not Guilty</u> of the <u>Specification</u>.

Of the <u>First Charge</u>: <u>Not Guilty</u>.

Of the <u>Specification</u> to the Second Charge: Referring to the opinion expressed under the kindred specification to the preceding Charge, the Court finds the Accused <u>Not Guilty</u> to the <u>Specification</u>

Of the <u>Second Charge</u>: <u>Not Guilty</u>.

The Court does hereby <u>acquit</u> the accused, Captain <u>Seth B. Thornton</u>, of the 2d Regiment of Dragoons.

C. F. Smith
Capt. 2d Art.
Judge Advocate

W J Worth
Bvt. Brig. Genl.

At 10' before 2 of the clock the court was adjourned to meet at 9 of the clock AM to-morrow.

Fifth Day

9 of the clock AM Thursday
July 16, 1846

The court met pursuant to adjournment. Present:

1. Brig. Gen. Worth
2. Lt. Col. Garland
3. Lt. Col. Childs
4. Lt. Col. Belknap
5. Lt. Col. Wilson
6. Major Lear
7. Major Graham
8. Major Allen
9. Major Abercrombie

Capt. Smith, Judge Advocate

Sitting with closed doors the proceedings of yesterday were read and the verdict signed.

C. F. Smith
Capt. 2d Art.
Judge Advocate

W J Worth
Bvt. Brig. Genl.

Court Martial
Matamoros Mex
July 11, 1846

Capt. Seth B. Thornton
2d Rgt Dragoons

Copy of proceedings
furnished Capt. Thornton
September 11, per his request on July 22

The opinion of the Court Martial in this case acquitting Capt. Thornton is approved.
<illegible signature>
August 4, 1846

Rc'd August 1, 1846

G. O. No. 35, Aug. 10, 1846

D

Defense of Capt.
S. B. Thornton, 2d
Dragoons

Mr. President and Gentlemen of the Court,

A long established principle of our profession and a stern sense of duty on the part of my accuser, I'm bound to believe, in justice to him and to myself, brings me before you as an unfortunate commander. Success, I am aware, is the criterion by which the military man is generally, if not always, to be judged. But even should I not be able to convince your minds that success was not wanting in the result of my expedition, yet I hope to establish, and feel confident in my ability to do it, that the failure is not attributable to any omission on my part of the "necessary and customary precautions."

On the night of the 24th of April last, I found myself charged with the execution of the instructions specified under the second charge upon which I am arraigned. My command, as officially reported to Col. Twiggs, my Regimental Commander, consisted of three commissioned officers and fifty one rank and file. The verbal instructions given me by the Commanding General according to his own testimony were very similar to if not identical with those in writing with the addition of requiring me to ascertain if practicable whether the enemy, if he had crossed, had artillery; and limiting me in time to 12 o'clock the next day. The manner in which I executed these instructions is so fully, and to my mind so satisfactorily explained in the testimony of Captain Hardee and Lt. Kane, witnesses for the prosecution, that I have deemed it unnecessary to call any of the numerous witnesses summoned for the defense. They only could and would have confirmed what is already before you. The want of any material witnesses, however, has prevented me from laying before the court in the strongest, most direct and most positive terms, the very minute and circumstantial instructions given by me to my advance guard when I learned that the enemy had probably crossed the river. My loss, however, whatever may be the consequences to myself, is insignificant when compared with that sustained by the Service, by the Country and by the friends of the noble and gallant <u>Mason</u>, who fell as he had lived, in the determined execution of his duty, regardless of all personal consequences except the preservation of that reputation which he has left as a rich inheritance to his friends.

The testimony of Captain Hardee upon nearly all matters connected with the squadron, previous to his entrance with it into the field where we were captured, is purely <u>negative</u>. His distance in my rear—150 or 200 yards—the darkness of the night and nature of the country, rendering it impossible for him to observe my movements or dispositions except such as related to himself with any precision.

It is clearly established by the testimony for the prosecution as well as defense that I marched about 9:00 on the night of the 24th of April, having thrown forward in advance guard under a non-comm'd officer, with which I placed my guide. That this advance guard, increased at a subsequent time, was kept out up to the time of entering the field where the squadron was captured. That "flankers," in the words of Captain Hardee, "were impossible at any time," "so thick was the country through which we passed." and, the "road, in almost its entire length, was a perfect defile, and so narrow in some places as to render it difficult for a single horseman to pass." Lieut. Kane, whose position with me at the head of the squadron enabled him to observe all that was done, says that "we moved taking the usual precautions of silence," that "orders were given by the commander of the squadron to prevent noise from the spurs even, and that these orders were frequently repeated and passed down the squadron." Captain Hardee, who had previously been over this portion of the road, says I inquired of him where a strong position could be found for a short rest, which I deemed necessary for my horses and men, and that when I halted for this rest I placed sentinels on the road in both directions so that no one could approach without my knowledge. Both he and Lieut. Kane agree as to the minute precautions that by me at this time to render a surprise impossible – requiring all my men to hold their bridles, and be ready to mount and move in case of any alarm. At this place I rested until near daylight thinking it imprudent to move, during the night, too near to an enemy of such force as was reported to have crossed the river, especially when he was perfectly acquainted with the country and I was most profoundly ignorant of it. About daylight I proceeded up the river with the same dispositions and precautions I had used the night before. Constant enquiries were made, says Captain Hardee; to ascertain if the enemy had crossed the river, and that I "was invariably told they had, but all spoke, as he believed, from rumors."

More than one member of this Court has had sufficient experience in Mexican duplicity to convince him that this was not reliable information. The false alarms which had occurred in our own camp for a month previous, through which the enemy's spies had passed unmolested, and even made drawings of our defenses, marking the positions of our Field Officers, and their names, with the strengths of their commands, were sufficient of themselves to make one receive with great caution any representations of their own as to the position or strength of their forces.

Deeming my dispositions prudent and safe, I moved on without changing them until I came upon three Mexicans at a "Rancho" some 10 miles from my resting place. Here the suspicious conduct of my guide caused me to doubt his fidelity, and subsequent events have but confirmed my suspicions. His desertion from our Army almost immediately after our capture, his reception and pardon in the Mexican Army, and his presence (which he has since confessed) upon the field of "Palo Alto," with General Arista, leave no doubt in my mind of his having been employed, in connection with other spies, to lead us, as they did, into a position from which retreat was impossible. One man, who was very officious in pointing out our route, left us when this guide did, and was afterwards recognized in uniform at the capture. Having learned at this house, as he no doubt did, with his whisperings with his accomplices, that his treachery was successful and his object attained, the guide determine on leaving me, for fear, as he said, of being killed by the Mexicans. If his fears of receiving justice at my hands, however, did not operate more strongly in bringing him to this conclusion than any he entertained for his own people with whom he has since united, then is he as much injured as I am deceived. Subsequent information of the most reliable character convinced us all that our return to camp was absolutely cut off at this time, the enemy having gained our rear with 500 Cavalry and more than 150 Indians. One of the strongest reasons for believing now that my guide was treacherous is the fact of his returning to our camp, without molestation from this force, and reporting our capture.

At this place I was told the enemy was near and in force, and the conduct of my guide giving me serious apprehensions, I increased my advance guard to a noncommissioned officer and 10 privates and placed it under the command of the Lieut. Mason. The most minute and positive instructions were given him to keep a quarter mile ahead of the squadron, to be vigilant and cautious in his movements, and to return and report to me should he see an enemy, after having reconnoitered him as far as consistent with safety, but in no event to fire until obliged to do so and then to fall back with all celerity for support. From this "Rancho" I moved without a guide, having failed in my endeavors to induce Chipito to proceed. My orders to Lieut. Mason were executed with judgment to my full and entire satisfaction. It may be said I ought to have returned from this point and reported to the Comdg. General what I had learned. But I submit to the Court whether I had yet gained reliable information on which to base a report. I had seen nothing of an enemy and no signs of one, and reports previously made to us, in a similar manner, have proven to be so totally incorrect that I dared not rely on these. I had learned nothing either of the enemy's strength or composition, and, in a word the object of my expedition had not been accomplished. From information since received it is made certain too, that an attempt to return from this place, even, would have proved more disastrous then did my more fortunate move forward.

From this point then I advanced, using every precaution in my power, having my carbines loaded and slung, ready for action, pistol priming examined and great coats taken off and strapped. Cautioning my command also that the enemy was near.

No rear guard was kept by me at any time during my march—none was prescribed in my instructions, and from its being much more unusual than either the advance guard or flankers, I take it for granted General Taylor would have prescribed it as he did them, had he deemed it at all necessary. With so small a command a rear guard would have been a most unusual and, as I conceive, improper disposition. But as it was possible the enemy might make his appearance in that direction, the rear was assigned as the permanent, as it was the tactical, position of the officer next in rank to myself. And according to his own testimony I never failed to order him back to his post whenever he left it, remarking to him that we knew not when we might be attacked. On reaching the field so often referred to, I assumed a position in the road where a path crossed and sent my advance guard to reconnoiter the river bank and discover if there were any entrance by the rear or any appearance of an enemy. On receiving a report that nothing was to be seen for a mile up and down and that the field could not be entered, I moved on, deeming it important to communicate with the people at the houses within this field, and that, if possible, gain some information from them, as my time was now very limited and I had not yet executed my orders in full. Just at this time I was informed of a horseman as having appeared in the road and retreated down a path leading back into the chaparral. I cautiously examine this path with my squadron, for a mile or more, and found, as I afterwards remarked to the Lieut. Kane, that about 500 Cavalry had passed there, adding that I believed they had gained our rear and that we should have to cut our way back to camp, giving him at the same time those minute instructions for his guidance in that event, which he has detailed to the Court. Finding this path was leading me into a marshy prairie where nothing was to be seen of the enemy, I determined to return and endeavor to gain information from the persons seen in the field if it could be done with safety. For that reason I left the head of my squadron and rode up to the advance guard. On arriving at the bars, I ordered them down and went in alone, determined not to risk the safety of an individual of my command by taking any of them into the field until it became necessary. Here the mixed nature of my duties required me to divest myself of the immediate military command of my squadron and to assume the character of reconnoitering officer. Had my orders to the squadron been strictly carried out it would not, says Lieut. Kane, have closed on the advance guard, and consequently, my signal made by a beckon for the guard to move on, would not have been seen by them.

The signal was made by me, without facing about, on seeing persons flying from the houses and believing I could only communicate by having them captured. Had the squadron permitted the advance guard to resume its proper distance, which I presumed as a matter of course it would permit it to keep, knowing my minute instructions on this point to Lieut. Mason were given in the presence and hearing of the Lieut. Kane who led the squadron, the latter never would have entered the field at all.

That I intended it should not do so, fully appears from my remark made on its first approach to me. The placing a sentinel at the bars was unnecessary unless I intended taking the squadron in. The throwing out a vidette or placing a sentinel ahead was totally unnecessary as the field was open to the sight, and the advance guard could not fail to discover any enemy in front in time to fall back on the main body at the bars. Besides, the country in front had already been examined and found perfectly clear. When the squadron reached me I was anxiously engaged in gaining information, and as the hour was late and my instructions required me to return by 12 o'clock that day, I had not a moment to lose, but was compelled in the exercise of my delicate duties as commander and reconnoitering officer to hasten my interview with the Mexicans and take up my march in return.

The conditions of the squadron at the time of the alarm, which seems to have been somewhat dwelt on by the prosecution, can under no circumstances be attributable to negligence on my part. So busily and so anxiously was I occupied, some 20 yards ahead of it, and facing from it, that I could not possibly give it my personal attention, and, in the words of Lieut. Kane, it is not at all probable that its condition came under my observation. That portion of my duties was necessarily left to my officers, who had received most positive instructions, and frequent cautions that the enemy was near, no precautions, however, at that time, for myself or any one else, could have altered the result—our fate was decided long before entering that field. An alarm being given, however, I executed the only move which offered the slightest hope of extrication from our perilous position. Seeing much the greater portion of my squadron in the saddle and close together, I ordered and executed a charge upon the enemy at the bars, the only opening, determined to fall in the attempt or, in the words of my instructions, to cut my way through the enemy. And expecting that the squadron might affect a passage through an opening I hoped to make by the superior power of my horse. Seeing the utter impossibility of this, on getting near enough to observe the immense strength of the enemy, and finding upon looking back that my men had swerved to the right and that their horses were almost unmanageable from the galling effect of the enemy's fire, I abandoned this idea and wheeled to the right also. My plan then was to skirt the fence for an opening; as none presented itself I ordered my men to dismount and tear down the fence in the face of the enemy, but such was now the condition of my command, produced by the destructive fire to which it was exposed, that I found it impossible to effect my purpose. My own horse was now almost unmanageable and I continued my route with a view of effecting an opening at some other point, but in a very few moments by horse fell, seriously wounded, and by the fall totally disabled me; besides falling on me in such a way as to render it extremely difficult for me to extricate myself after having partially recovered from the severe shock which I had received.

In reviewing the whole facts of the case then, gentlemen, as developed by the testimony on your record: it appears that I was charged, not only with the military command of my squadron of dragoons, but with the still more delicate and responsible duty of reconnoitering the enemy, for the purpose of discovering his positions, his strength and his composition. I had to examine a most difficult country of twenty seven miles in extent and return to camp in the short space of <u>fifteen hours,</u> eight of which were in the night. I was examining a country of the most difficult nature, with which I was totally unacquainted and which was correctly supposed to be in the possession of an enemy perfectly familiar with it. In doing this, I had to combine the two almost inconsistent if not totally incompatible characters of reconnoitering officer and commander of his military escort. For my guide, I had a citizen of the enemy's country, of doubtful fidelity at best, and who communicated with them in a language wholly unknown to me. Such was the nature of the country that it is the opinion of the officers who were with me, that my rear might have been easily gained by day, as it was by night, without the possibility of me knowing it. And that an attempt to return would have been followed by total and inevitable destruction. The enemy had spies upon us from the moment of our starting to the time of our capture. Indeed, they had full information of this, as they always had before it, of every movement of our army. Such were the relations which we sustained toward them that concealment on our part was impossible, whilst the slightest attempt to gain information of them was hazardous in the extreme. Our little army was compelled under its instructions, to keep up a peaceable attitude until the first blow should be given by them. It was my misfortune to receive that first blow up on my devoted head; but it had to be received, and why not by me? I contend then that the result of my expedition was not disastrous. Nearly half of a squadron of Dragoons were captured, I admit; but what signifies that when compared with the immense advantage to a Commanding General, of knowing his real position, of being confident he no longer occupied debatable ground, of being certain the enemy were gaining his rear in force and determined to give him battle. If this was not important information, why the immediate requisition for heavy re-inforcements? Why the redoubled activity in the completion of Fort Brown? Why the sudden and rapid move upon Point Isabel for ammunition and provisions?

But for the loss of this squadron, gentlemen, for which I am called on to atone, the thanks of a grateful people might never have been tendered to the "Heroes of Palo Alto and Resaca de la Palma." But, instead of tears of destitute widows and the cries of helpless orphans might have been answered as they heretofore been with cold indifference in the halls of our National legislature. Rather than such should be the case I would willingly conceal in my breast again, however painful and difficult the task, the only bleeding heart amidst the rejoicing of a victorious army.

If, gentlemen, I neglected any necessary or usual precautions to secure my command, it must have resulted from a want of knowledge. And I pray you, therefore, the acquit me of the <u>neglect,</u> and, if necessary, render your verdict against me for incapacity. I had hoped, however, that a successful service, known to some of this Court, with several campaigns, in Florida, against an enemy, at least as treacherous and wily as the Mexicans, would have enabled me, in the performance of my duties here, to defy such an imputation. If I had disobeyed an order, it is the first time in my life, and I hope I am not too sanguine in concluding that literal obedience in this instance was impossible, and its attempt inevitable destruction.

Mr. President and Gentleman, my military reputation – my honor—my all—is committed to your keeping. Your country has found hers safe in your hands, and, with the confidence which that is calculated to inspire, I submit my case to your decision.

Matamoros Mexico
July 13, 1846

S. B. Thornton
Captain 2d Reg. dragoons

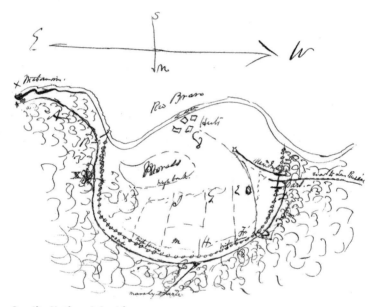

Credit: National Archives

Rough sketch of
"Caracita"
the farm where Capt.
Thornton's squadron
was defeated and captured
April 25/46

Notes

CHAPTER 1

1. All anecdotes, details, and quotes in this chapter concerning the events of Thornton's patrol, unless otherwise specified, are from NARA 1790449 (Hardee court of inquiry) and NARA 1790477 (Thornton court-martial). The full transcripts are in Appendixes D and E.

2. Horse data is from War Department FM2-15, on the assumption that horses had not changed since 1846.

3. Republic of the Rio Grande Museum, Webb County Heritage Foundation.

4. Rodenbough, 115–16.

5. Katcher, 16.

6. Chartrand, 18.

7. Katcher, 3.

8. Biographical data in the following paragraphs is from Heitman, various entries.

9. Unattributed, Vol. 2, 171–73.

10. Rodenbough, 99.

CHAPTER 2

1. Goode, 398.

2. MacGregor, correspondence with author.

3. Information about the Thornton family is from Ancestry.com.

4. MacGregor.

5. Goode, 399.

6. MacGregor.

7. Heitman, Thornton's entry.

8. Rodenbough, 22.

9. Rodenbough, 24.

10. Gardner, Thornton's entry.

11. Heitman, Thornton's entry.

12. NARA, "Returns from U.S. Military Posts," various entries.

13. *North Carolina Standard*, June 27, 1838.

14. McLeod, 95.

15. US House of Representatives, Rochester entry.

16. Unattributed, Vol. 2, 173.

17. Ancestry.com has the Twiggs family tree. There were seven siblings, including George Lowe Twiggs (1789–1853), David Emanuel Twiggs (1790–1862), and Levi Twiggs (1793–1847).

18. *Augusta Constitutionalist*, May 19, 1853, posted in Ancestry.com.

19. *Augusta Chronicle*, October 14, 1999.

20. Fort Wiki, Fort Braden entry.

21. NARA, identifier 1788675, enclosure A.

22. Ap is a Welsh patronymic. Jones should not be confused with his son, Catesby ap Roger Jones, later commander of the ironclad CSS *Virginia*.

23. Details of the incident are from the court-martial file, NARA 1786857.

24. Wikipedia, Thomas T. Fauntleroy entry, mentioned a War of 1812 commission, without attribution.

25. Heitman, Robert G. Asheton entry.

26. Heitman, Thornton's entry.

27. Department of State, 56–57.

28. Wright, various pages.

29. Rodenbough, 60–61.

30. Rodenbough, 70.

31. Rodenbough, 39.

32. Hughes, 21.

33. NARA, Returns from U.S. Military Posts.

34. Details of the incidents of April 1843 and of the resulting court-martial and its documents are from the court-martial file, NARA 1788675.

35. Rodenbough, 19.

36. NARA, Returns from U.S. Military Posts.

Chapter 3

1. Kohl, 12.

2. Mayer, Chapter 2.

3. Scheina, 44.

4. Grant, 54.

5. Eisenhower, 32–33.

6. Incidents are from Captain Thornton's court of inquiry file, NARA Identifier 1790308.

7. Rodenbough, 20.

8. Bauer, Chapter 3.

9. Tenenbaum, 182.

10. DePalo, 94.

11. DePalo, 99.

12. Risch, 245.
13. Ibid.
14. Author estimates, based on multiple maps.
15. Negrete, Chapter 4, throughout.

CHAPTER 4
1. Details are from the Thornton trial and Hardee court of inquiry transcripts. See Appendixes D and E.
2. Rodenbough, 101.
3. Wikipedia, George Thomas Mason entry.
4. Murphy, data, for all the enlisted men.

CHAPTER 5
1. House Executive Documents, 288.
2. Eisenhower, 66–68.
3. House Executive Documents, 290.
4. Rodenbough, throughout.
5. Negrete, 146, translated by Tim O'Donnell.
6. House Executive Documents, 289–90.

CHAPTER 6
1. Rodenbough, 99.
2. House Executive Documents, 288–89.
3. Haecker and Mauck, 26–27.
4. Grant, 95.
5. Rodenbough, 516.
6. Rodenbough, 441.
7. Carney, 22.
8. DePalo, 102. His text misplaces Linares.

CHAPTER 7
1. Winders, 53.
2. Rodenbough, 100.

CHAPTER 8
1. Rodenbough, 432.
2. Esposito, map 15.
3. Eisenhower, 257.
4. Details about that afternoon concerning Captain Thornton are from his court-martial file, NARA 1791090.
5. Eisenhower, 296.
6. Movement details from Esposito, Vol. 1, 15–16.

7. Bauer, 284.
8. Rodenbough, 151.
9. War Department, *Ordnance Manual*, 387.
10. Unattributed, Vol. 2, 172–73.
11. Rodenbough, 152.

CHAPTER 9

1. Bauer, 318.
2. Bauer, 388.
3. *Brownsville Herald*, "Game Over," October 5, 2015.
4. O.R., Series I, Vol. 4, Chapter 13, Item 1.
5. *Appletons' Cyclopædia*, T. T. Fauntleroy entry.
6. Wikipedia, Charles A May entry.
7. Heitman, Elias Kent Kane entry.
8. Wikipedia, David E. Twiggs entry.
9. Gardner, Twiggs entries.
10. Wikipedia, Mariano Arista entry.
11. Krauze, 151.
12. Hughes, throughout.

CHAPTER 10

1. Krauze, 767–68.

CHAPTER 11

1. Murphy.

CHAPTER 12

1. NSDAR
2. Author inspection, July 2013.
3. Rodenbough, 432.
4. Google Maps, various views, accessed in November 2015.
5. Perttula, throughout.
6. Garza, "Carricitos," accessed November 17, 2015.
7. Garza, "Las Rusias," accessed November 17, 2015.
8. State Department, Boundary Commission, plate 21.

APPENDIX B

1. DePalo, 96.
2. Haecker, 212.

APPENDIX C

1. Murphy, data.

Bibliography

Ancestry.com, various collections.

Appletons' Cyclopædia of American Biography. New York: D. Appleton and Co., 1900. Available at https://en.wikisource.org/wiki/Appletons'_Cyclop%C3%A6dia_of_ American_Biography, accessed February 4, 2016.

Augusta Chronicle, archives (for October 14, 1999). http://old.chronicle.augusta.com/ stories/1999/10/14/met_273000.shtml, accessed January 1, 2016.

Bauer, K. Jack. *The Mexican War, 1846-1848*. New York: Macmillan, 1974.

Brownsville Herald. Available at www.brownsvilleherald.com, accessed February 5, 2016.

Carney, Stephen A. *Guns Along the Rio Grande*. US Army Center of Military History, 2005. Available at www.history.army.mil//html/books/073/73-2/index.html, accessed January 27, 2016.

Chartrand, Rene. *Santa Anna's Mexican Army 1821–48*. Oxford: Osprey Publishing, 2004.

DePalo, William A. *The Mexican National Army, 1822–1852*. College Station: Texas A&M University Press, 1997.

Department of State. *Register of All Officers and Agents, Civil, Military, and Naval, in the Service of the United States on the Thirtieth of September 1845*. Washington, DC: Gideon Printers, 1845.

Eisenhower, John S. D. *So Far From God, the U.S. War with Mexico, 1846–1848*. New York: Random House, 1989.

Esposito, Brig. Gen. Vincent J. *West Point Atlas of American Wars*. New York: Praeger Publishers, 1959.

Fort Wiki, www.fortwiki.com, accessed January 4, 2016.

Gardner, Charles K. *A Dictionary of All Officers Who Have Been Commissioned or Have Been Appointed and Served in the Army of the United States to 1853*, Second Edition. New York: Van Nostrand, 1860.

Garza, Alicia A. "Carricitos, TX." *Handbook of Texas Online*. www.tshaonline.org/ handbook/online/articles/hnc16), accessed November 17, 2015. Uploaded on June 12, 2010. Published by the Texas State Historical Association.

———. "Las Rusias, TX." *Handbook of Texas Online*. www.tshaonline.org/handbook/ online/articles/hrlcs), accessed November 17, 2015. Uploaded on June 15, 2010. Published by the Texas State Historical Association.

Goode, G. Brown. *Virginia Cousins*. Richmond, VA: Clearfield, 1887.

Grant, Ulysses S. *Personal Memoirs of U.S. Grant*. New York: Charles L. Webster & Co., 1885.

Haecker, Charles M. *A Thunder of Cannon: Archeology of the Mexican-American War Battlefield of Palo Alto*. Santa Fe, NM: National Park Service, 1994.

Haecker, Charles M., and Jeffrey G. Mauck. *On the Prairie of Palo Alto, Historical Archeology of the U.S.–Mexican War Battlefield*. College Station: Texas A&M University Press, 1997.

Heitman, Francis B. *Historical Register and Dictionary of the United States Army from its Organization, September 29, 1789, to March 2, 1903*. Washington, DC: Government Printing Office, 1903.

House Executive Documents, 30th Congress, 1st Session. US House of Representatives (Ex. Doc. No. 60), Library of Congress, available at https://memory.loc.gov/cgi-bin/ampage?collId=llss&fileName=0500/0520/llss0520.db&recNum=14, accessed January 21, 2016.

Hughes, Nathanial C. *General William J. Hardee, Old Reliable*. Baton Rouge: Louisiana State University Press, 1965.

Katcher, Philip. *The Mexican-American War 1846–48*. Oxford: Osprey Publishing, 1989.

Kohl, Clayton Charles. *Claims As a Cause of the Mexican War*. New York: New York University, 1914. Available at www.archive.org/stream/cu31924020403477/ cu31924020403477_djvu.txt, accessed January 29, 2016.

Krauze, Enrique. *Mexico: Biography of Power*. New York: HarperCollins Publishers, 1997.

Lambert, Joseph Idus. *One Hundred Years with the Second Cavalry*. Fort Riley, KS: Capper Printing Co., 1939. Text available at http://history.dragoons.org/category/ seminole-war/, accessed November 24, 2015.

MacGregor, Jerrilynn Eby. Stafford County (VA) Historical Society, secretary. Personal correspondence with author. Background information at http://staffordhistorical .org, accessed March 2, 2016.

Mayer, Brantz. *History of the War Between Mexico and the United States, with a Preliminary View of Its Origin, Volume 1*. New York: Wiley and Putnam, 1848. Available at www.gutenberg.org/ebooks/33568, accessed January 29, 2016.

McLeod, Mrs. Hugh (nee Lamar, Rebecca). "The Loss of the Steamer *Pulaski*." *Georgia Historical Quarterly*, Vol. 3, No. 2 (June 1919), 63–95.

Murphy, Douglas A. Palo Alto National Battlefield, staff historian and administrator. Database access, e-mails, and conversations with author.

National Archives and Records Administration (NARA), Washington, DC. Record Group 153: Records of the Office of the Judge Advocate General (Army).

———. 24 December, 1840, Court Martial of 1st Lt. S. B. Thornton, Box 114, Case File CC551, National Archives Identifier 1786857.

———. 29 May, 1843, Court Martial of Capt. S. B. Thornton: Box 128, Case File DD271, National Archives Identifier 1788675.

———. 28 August, 1845, Court of Inquiry for Capt. S. B. Thornton, Box 148, Case File EE203, National Archives Identifier 1790308.

———. 26 May, 1846, Court of Inquiry of Capt. W. J. Hardee, Case File EE248, National Archives Identifier 1790449.

———. 10 July, 1846, Court Martial of Capt. Seth B. Thornton, Case File EE255, National Archives Identifier 1790477.

———. 29 May, 1847, Court Martial of Capt. Seth B. Thornton, Box 156, Case File EE419, National Archives Identifier 1791090.

NARA. Miscellaneous documents, as cited.

———. "Returns from U.S. Military Posts, 1800–1916." Records of the Adjutant General's Office, 1780s–1917, Record Group 94; accessed through Ancestry.com, December 22, 2015.

Negrete, Emilio del Castillo. *Invasion de los Norte-Americanos en México*. Mexico: Imprenta del Editor, 1890.

North Carolina Standard, June 27, 1838, page 3. Available online through the Library of Congress, http://chroniclingamerica.loc.gov/lccn/sn85042147/1838-06-27/ed-1/seq-3/, accessed January 1, 2016.

NSDAR. Lt. Thomas Barlow Chapter, San Benito, Texas, http://www.texasdar.org/chapters/LieutenantThomasBarlow/, accessed November 13, 2015.

Official Army Records of the War of the Rebellion (O.R.). Washington, DC: War Department, 1901.

Perttula, Timothy K., et al. *Rancho de Carricitos, or Thornton's Skirmish, Archeological Investigations. . .* Brownsville, TX: National Park Service, 1997.

Republic of the Rio Grande Museum, Webb County Heritage Foundation. http://webbheritage.org/museums/republic-of-the-rio-grande-museum/, accessed October 20, 2015.

Risch, Erna. *Quartermaster Support of the Army: A History of the Corps 1775–1939*. Washington, DC: Quartermaster Historian's Office, Office of the Quartermaster General, 1962.

Rodenbough, Theophilus F. *From Everglades to Cañon with the Second United States Cavalry*. New York: D. Van Nostrand, 1875. (The Second Dragoons was renamed the Second Cavalry in 1861.)

Scheina, Robert L. *Santa Anna: A Curse Upon Mexico*. Washington, DC: Brassey's Inc., 2002.

State Department. "Proceedings of the International (Water) Boundary Commission." Washington, DC: Government Printing Office, 1903.

Tenenbaum, Barbara. *The Politics of Penury, Debts and Taxes in Mexico, 1821–1856*. Albuquerque: University of New Mexico Press, 1986.

Texas Tribune. Available at www.texastribune.org, accessed February 5, 2016.

Unattributed. *The Mexican War and Its Heroes*. Philadelphia: Grigg, Eliott and Co., 1849.

US House of Representatives. "Biographical Directory of the United States Congress," http://bioguide.congress.gov/scripts/biodisplay.pl?index=R000360, accessed December 22, 2015.

War Department. *FM2-15, Cavalry Field Manual, Employment of Cavalry.* Washington, DC: Government Printing Office, 1941.

———. *Ordnance Manual, 1862.* Philadelphia: J. B. Lippincott & Co., 1861.

Wikipedia, sections as cited, accessed in 2015 and 2016.

Winders, Richard Bruce. *Mr. Polk's Army: The American Military Experience in the Mexican War.* College Station: Texas A&M University Press, 1997.

Wright, Carroll D. *Comparative Wages, Prices, and Cost of Living.* Boston: Wright & Potter Printing Co., 1889. Accessed through Google Books, March 2, 2016.

Index

About the Author

Lamont Wood has written about the Trans-Nueces War for *Armchair General Magazine*. He has been freelancing for more than thirty years, has written ten books under his own name and has ghost-written several others. He has also written hundreds of articles for scores of magazines and newspapers, including *Scientific American*, the *Christian Science Monitor*, the *Chicago Tribune*, *InformationWeek*, *Computerworld*, *Network World*, *Datamation*, *LiveScience.com*, the old *Byte* and *Omni*, and magazines in Canada, England, Holland, Belgium, Germany, and Hong Kong. History magazines he has written for include *World at War*, *Strategy & Tactics*, *Armchair General*, and *True West*.